Cover girl: Jo Guest

THE INDISPENSABLE GUIDE
FOR HEDONISTS

First published 1996

Revised July 1999

THIS IS A *Niche* PUBLICATION

Contents

Contents

Acknowledgements

The Editor
Richard de Clare has been a publisher and editor for over twenty years, during which time he has produced guides and publications for the Ladbroke and Hilton Group of hotels. He has also edited the monthly magazines, The Theatre Visitor and London After Dark and has contributed to The Daily Express and the London Evening Standard.

Acknowledgements
The author and publishers would like to thank the following for their boundless energy and invaluable advice in researching the information contained in this guide: Michael Stewart, David Parker, Desmond Robinson, Paul Kilkenny, Roland Blunk, Stephen Turnham, Nicholas Creagh-Osborne, Hubert Gieschen, Sheila Aspinall, Brian Jenner, The LTCB and the Society of London Theatre Watchdog Distribution; Distribution (Ireland):Shane Flynn, Distribution (France): WH Smith and Eurostar; Joel Reed 150 West 58 Street New York. Photographs by: Alec Gerry, Steve Wood and Michael le Poer Trench.

Night Out in London
Night Out in London is compiled and published by:
Niche Publications Limited, P.O.Box 20988, 31 London Street, London W2 3GX
Telephone: +44(0)171 402 1946 Facsimile: +44(0)171 402 4161
Website: http: www.ndirect.co.uk/~declare/ ; e:mail: declare@ndirect.co.uk

Whilst every care has been taken to obtain accurate and reliable information at the time of going to press, it should be emphasised that opening times may alter, management, staff, and venue names can change at very short notice.

Liability
The publishers cannot accept liability for any errors or omissions in this publication but will gladly incorporate any suggestions for improvement or any inaccuracies in the next edition.
Printed by Cambrian Printers Aberystwyth; Photosetting: Capital Graphics.
ISBN 0 9532299 0 4

Welcome to Night Out in London - the only guide of its kind covering all aspects of night- life in 'our wonderful city. This indispensable companion has now been in existence for three years, and our readership continues to grow. Distribution has now been extended to Paris, Amsterdam and New York and stocks are 'available in all the shops of the Four and Five Star hotels in the Capital.

This is our first full-colour issue, giving you a complete insight into the bright lights - including an extensive guide to the latest craze for lapdancing. Venues for this exotic X-rated activity are mushrooming, and our researchers have been quick to spot the divas from the dollies.

London is amaze of undiscovered treats. There is plenty here for the inexperienced visitor seeking the sophistication of Covent Garden or a bit of sleaze from Streatham. We also look out for the local businessman anxious to widen his knowledge of the lairs and lanes of the pullulating metropolis. But not forgetting the ladies - we have details of beauty treatments, hairdressers and even matchmakers.

There are short articles giving honest appraisals of nightime entertainment, together with easily- referenced listings, which will help you to find your way around. Elsewhere, we have an up-to-the-minute list of pubs, clubs, restaurants and bars. The restaurants are carefully reviewed to reassure you of a pleasant meal in the right atmosphere. Judging by the reader response, you're taking our recommendations and enjoying everything from the gay bars to the greyhound racing.

We review the 'jazz haunts, the techo and the salsa and, not to mention, the big showpiece musicals. You'll find a special section on stag nights, tips for the best live comedy performances and a chapter devoted to 'before the night begins'. You'll also be able to find an internet cafe, so you can broadcast your wild and unusual experiences to your friends and family back home.

The boom in London goes on and on and we hope we can put the 'fizz' into your Friday and the 'wow' into your weekend! And remember if you make any of your own discoveries - tell us and we'll tell everyone else in our next edition. Have Fun.

Before the Night Begins

Spending the night out on the tiles, painting the town red, or just going to your 'local', is not always as straight-forward as it sounds. It can be a spontaneous decision or it may involve a fair amount of planning.

If you have children, you may need a babysitter. If you are going somewhere formal you may require the services of a clothes hire firm. If you are travelling you need to know the train times and prices.

Taxis are often a requirement if you want to leave the car behind for fear of being clamped, or indeed breathalysed, if you have one or two glasses of wine with your meal.

Why not take the Party Bus, (telephone: 0171 630 6063) which claims to be the first mobile night-club? Tour price includes free admission into four of London's top night clubs in the same evening. They also offer a 'free pick up' and 'drop-off' service for groups anywhere in the home counties. The double-decker bus is complete with resident DJ on board and a commercial PA/sound system.

If you are a woman on your own and a trifle nervous of hiring a minicab driven by a male, in these crime-ridden days, the firm for you is Lady Cars. This is a company which is for women only with only women drivers. They now have two branches in North London with over sixty drivers but cover most areas, providing that you make your reservation in advance.

Currency

British currency is based on a £1 sterling unit, divided into 100 pence (p). The coins have values ranging from 1p to £2. Bank notes range from £5 (blue), the £10 is brown, £20 (purple) and £50 (red). The £50 notes are uncommon, and if you are not collecting them from a bank they should be avoided.

Getting Around on Foot

Although many Londoners choose to ignore them, it is best to cross the street using using zebra crossings, where pedestrians have priority, or underground passages /subways. Some outer areas are unsafe after nightfall. If outside the city centre after dark stick to the high streets whenever possible.

Rush Hours

The rush hours are approximately from 8-9.30am and 5-7pm Monday-Friday. Unlike some cities, London does not become totally choked but the situation is getting so, since shopping is now a seven- day- a -week activity.

Customs and Etiquette

The English are a tolerant people and London is a cosmopolitan city, so visitors are unlikely to offend by tripping up on some part of etiquette. An important custom is 'queuing' - the British queue for everything and it is advisable to wait your turn in order to avoid a serious verbal attack.

Tipping

Tipping is customary in a few cases. A tip of between 10-15 per cent tends to be the norm. Hotels and restaurants usually include the service charge in the bill. Taxi drivers generally expect the average tip, as well as porters, hairdressers, lavatory attendants and doormen who also need to be rewarded.

Telephone

Most telephone boxes use all English coins from 10p upwards. You will also find 'card phones' available which can be more convenient, especially for long distance and overseas calls. The phone cards can be bought from post offices or newsagents. Do not buy from street traders and check that the packet is securely sealed.

Renting a car

It is probably not worthwhile if you do not intend to go outside London. You must be over 21 and hold a full valid national licence. You can either opt for a daily rate plus a mileage charge or a weekly rate with unlimited mileage, often more economical.

Parking

Parking meters take a variety of coins depending on the area in which you are trying to park. A great many areas have a 'Pay and Display' system, where you place money in a nearby machine and receive a ticket which must be placed in a visible position in the car, ideally inside the front windscreen.

Banking hours

Most banks are open from 9.30am to 4.30pm on Mondays to Fridays except Bank Holidays. Some also open on Saturday mornings until 12.30pm. 24-hours facilities are available. At Heathrow. Banking is also available between 5.30am to 9pm at: Thomas Cook, Victoria Station SW1.

Visitors information

For details of sights or other events: London Tourist Board information service -Tel: 0171 730 3488 (Mon – Fri 9.am – 5.30pm.) The Information Centre is on Victoria Station forecourt, SW1. The leaflets on offer will help with arranging excursions and are available from multi-lingual staff. It is open every day from 8am to 7pm Easter to October, and Monday to Saturday 8 am to 6pm (Sunday 9am to 4pm) November to Easter. The London Tourist Board operates a comprehensive range of recorded information services available 24 hours a day on Visitorcall.

The information is updated daily and can be obtained by dialling 0839 123, followed by the number given for each category: ie Current Exhibitions 403, West End Shows 416, New Productions & how to book 438, Rock & Pop Concerts 422. Calls charged at 39p per minute cheap rate, 49p per minute at all other times, plus any hotel/payphone surcharge.

PICCADILLY

Travel within London

Buses and Underground (Tube) railway services operate throughout the week from around 6am-12.30am depending on the individual route. For information about times and prices telephone London Transport 0171 222 1234. If you plan to do several journeys on any one day or use the Underground frequently, it will prove easier and cheaper to buy a daily or weekly travel pass. These travel passes are available from stations or some newsagents. You can, of course, also hire a car which is particularly convenient if you plan to travel outside of London.

Travel within London

At most mainline terminals there is usually a taxi rank, or you can hail a cab in the street. An orange sign is lit up when the taxi is free; remember that demand exceeds supply when there is a sudden down-pour, strike, or in the rush hour. Charges are according to fixed metered rates, with surcharges for distances over six miles, two or more passengers, evening journeys and extra baggage.

Going By Rail

London has seven main rail stations at which Intercity express trains terminate. These are spread around the centre of town. Paddington in West London serves the West country, Wales and the South Midlands. Liverpool Street in the City serves East Anglia and Essex. In North London Euston, St. Pancras and Kings Cross cover Northern, Central England and Scotland whilst Victoria and Waterloo link the whole of Southern England.

Black Cabs/Cars

Computer Cab	0171 286 0286
Radio Taxi cabs	0171 272 0272
Dial-a-Cab	0171 253 5000
Lady Cabs	0171 254 3501
L.A Stretch Limos:	0181 923 9988

One for the Road

Tel: 0171 924 4141
Opening hours: Mon-Wed until 1am
Thu-Sat until 3.30am
This relatively new service offers a solution if you have driven your car and find yourself over the limit. They send a driver on a fold up motorbike who drives to your destination and puts his/her bike in a fold- up- bag. They then drive your car home saving you the cost of two taxi journeys and retrieval costs the following morning. The minimum cost is £10 charged on any journey up to three miles. £3 a mile up to 8 miles and this reduces to £2 a mile thereafter. The drivers are insured to drive cars worth up to the value of £75,000.

Babysitters

It is always a worry leaving your children with complete strangers but both Babysitters Unlimited and Childminders have been in business for some years and vet all their staff very carefully - most of whom are trained nurses.

Babysitters Unlimited

2 Napoleon Road Twickenham
Tel: 0181 892 8888
The agency was first established in 1967. It has been in the hands of Judy Thomas, the present owner, since 1980 and most of the staff have worked for the agency since that time.

Childminders

Established 1967
6 Nottingham Street Baker Street W1
Tel: 0171 935 3000
24 hour info line: 0171 487 5040
Nearly all the sitters are drawn from nurses, nannies and teachers and all are personally interviewed and references are thoroughly checked before being employed.

Dress and Party Hire

Frock Around the Clock
42 Vardens Gardens SW11
Tel: 0171 924 1669
Full range of cocktail party dresses
with matching accessories which can
either be bought or hired.

Panto Box
26 North Street SW4
Tel: 0171 627 1772
Open Mon-Fri by appointment.
Supply animal costumes, diamante
jewellery, ball masks, as well as make-
up, wigs and head gear. A minimum
charge of £37.50 will get you a basic
outfit.

The Costume Studio
6 Panton Street Islington N1
Tel: 0171 388 4481
This is a truly excellent little shop.
They offer a very fine, value for money
service specialising in period and
theatrical costumes.

Angels
119 Shaftesbury Avenue WC2
Tel: 0171 836 5678
Probably the biggest costumiers in the
country, supplying most of the
television and film companies. They
also have a private hire department
that is more expensive than most, but
the choice is enormous

Hairdressers

Stage Door
16 Drury Lane Covent Garden WC2
Tel: 0171 240 8384
Open Mon- Fri 9.30am- 7.15;
Sat 9.30am-5.45
Situated in the heart of theatreland
this award winning salon specialises
in cutting, colour and extensive hair-
care.

Nicky Clarke
130 Mount Street Mayfair W1
Tel: 0171 491 4700
They say that a haircut by Nicky
Clarke in his swish Mayfair salon can
cost the same price as a holiday in
Thailand. Nevertheless, the leather-
trousered coiffeur has no shortage of
clients. Among his most famous are:
the Duchess of York, Patsy Kensit and
Posh Spice Victoria Adams. If you
want Nicky's personal attention, you
will have to join the three month or
so waiting-list.

Hairdressers

Antenna

27d Kensington Church Street W8
Tel: 0171 938 1866
Open Mon-Wed 9.30am-6.30pm;
Thu-Fri 9.30am-9pm;
Sat 9.30am-6.30pm
This salon is best known for its hair-extensions. They also cut and colour as well as perm.

Daniel Field

8-12 Broadwick Street W1
Tel: 0171 439 8223
Open Tue 10am-8pm; Wed 10am-5.30pm; Thu 10am-8pm; Fri 10am-6.30pm; Sat 9am-4pm

The pioneer of 'organic and mineral' hairdressing. The salon also specialises in colour. Daniel no longer takes bookings but his assistant Bradley charges £50 for a cut, with a full head of highlights costing £120.

Daniel Oliver

7 The Arcade Dolphin Square SW1
Tel: 071 834 4595
Cut and blow dry costs:
(Ladies) £30; (Gentlemen) £15.00
Open Mon-Fri 9am-6pm;
Sat 8.30am- 2pm (No credit cards).
Small but centrally located salon specialising in traditional hair styles.

Edward's Hair & Beauty

Grosvenor House Hotel
Park Lane W1
Tel: 0171 491 7875
(Ladies) £45; (Gentlemen) £26.00
5 stylists and 3 beauty therapists
Open Mon-Sat 9am-6pm; Fri 9-7pm

Have been resident in The Grosvenor House for over 25 years offering general hair and beauty treatments.

Hairdressers

Hugh and Stephen
161 Ebury Street
Victoria SW1
Tel: 0171 730 2196
Open Mon-Fri 9am- 5pm
Average cost £87
Mainly a residential salon but boasts of having members of the Royal family as clients. Have been established for 24 years.

Molton Brown
54 Rosslyn Hill
Hampstead NW3
Tel: 0171 794 2022
Open Mon Wed 10am-6pm; Thu-Fri 10am-7pm; Sat 9am-5pm
Creative cutting and colouring the natural way on long and short hair. Hand-drying techniques a speciality.

Trevor Sorbie
10 Russell Street
Covent Garden WC2
Tel: 0171 379 6901
Open Mon -Tue 9am-6pm; Wed 9am-7.00pm; Thu & Fri 9am-7.40 pm; Sat 9am-5pm
This popular salon specialises in cutting and colouring.

Vidal Sassoon
60 South Molton Street W
Tel: 0171-491 8848
Open Mon-Wed 8.30am-5.45pm; Thu 6.30pm; Fri & Sat 8.45am-5pm
You know the cut and if you like the style, this is the place for you.

Hari's Hairdressers
305 Brompton Road SW3
Tel: 0171 581 5211
Open 10am-6.15pm Mon to Sat
Have been established for over sixteen years. The salon is extremely busy and popular with people from the world of show-business. A two day advance booking period is highly recommended.

Barbers

Sweeney's
48 Beauchamp Place
Knightsbridge SW3
Tel: 0171 589 3066
Even though it is recognised as a barber shop it claims to be more of a unisex salon. The owner, Gavin Hodge, says 'all our clients are celebrities and we always have exceedingly attractive girls to wash our gentlemen's hair'. The salon has a loyal following with a cut and blow dry costing around £25.

G F Trumper
9 Curzon Street Mayfair W1
Tel: 0171 499 1850
Have three shops in Central London and offer the customer the ultimate barber shop experience. From the time your bottom hits the chair you feel that you are in a time warp. Haircut and shampoo around £24 and a shave with hot towels from £17.50.

Austin Reed
103/113 Regent Street W1
Tel: 0171 734 6789
Established 1930.
Tucked away in the basement of this famous store and close to Piccadilly Circus you can relax from shopping by having a haircut and shampoo at around £25.00.

Fitness Clubs

within the London area and stylists are available for bookings and consultations through out the week.

Memberships are currently available at five Livingwell clubs within Central London. Call us to arrange a personalised tour of the club and let us cater for your requirements:

Maida Vale Premier	0171 379 3232
Millbank Premier	0171 233 3579
Russell Square Premier	0171 291 6500
Langham Hilton	0171 973 7575
Park Lane Hilton	0171 629 6974

LivingWell have a reputation as friendly, 'members only' health and fitness clubs with an emphasis on the 'personal touch'. Conveniently, Livingwell members can use over 66 clubs nationwide and are provided with complimentary towels, toiletries, lockers and studio classes. Turn you ruin back into a temple or just balance your hectic lifestyle? Qualified instructors and personal trainers are on hand to offer help and advice or structure personalised exercise programmes to your specifications. All in a relaxed yet professional environment. Unisex swimming pools, spas, saunas and steam rooms are provided for lounging, socialising and relaxation. Combine these aspects with a stress relieving Swedish or Alternative Therapy massage in the Beauty department and your recovery from the night before can be swift and pampered instead of slow and torturous! Macmillans, the renowned Covent Garden hair salon, has branches at LivingWell Premier clubs

Champneys

Le Meridien 21 Piccadilly W1
Tel: 0171 437 8114
Open Mon-Fri 7am-11pm; Sat and Sun 8am-9pm

Facilities include 12 metre swimming pool, gym, cardiovascular room, two glass-backed squash courts, spa, dance studio, restaurant and drawing room. Various membership categories are available, including corporate day programmes.

Lambton Place Club

Lambton Place Westbourne Grove W11
Tel: 0171 229 2291
Open-Mon-Fri 7am-11pm
Sat and Sun 9am-9pm

A magnificent hi-tech gym with superb indoor swimming pool, spa sauna and steam rooms. Membership is on request. Squash and Tennis are on offer at their sister club, The Hogarth. The joining fee here is £250 and the 'gold card facility' is approximately £125 per month.

Shake that body

The Porchester Centre
Porchester Road Bayswater W2
Tel: 0171 792 2919
The centre is fully geared with all
the latest 'State of the Art' Cybex
equipment. The Hi-Tec cardiovascular
includes Liferowers, Lifecycles,
Lifesteps and treadmills. Various
packages are on offer once you have
completed the induction course.

The Ragdale Clinic at Michaeljohn
25 Albemarle Street W1
Tel: 0171 409 2956
Open:Mon & Sat 8.30am-6.30pm
Tue-Fri 8.30am-8.30pm
In addition to their massages and sun
beds, Ultra-bronze £20 for 20 minutes
and aromatherapy from £50 for
ninety minutes.

The Sanctuary Ladies Only Club
12 Floral Street Covent Garden WC2
Tel: 0171 420 5151
Sat-Tue 10am-6.00pm
Wed-Fri 10am-10.00pm
Tanya and Allan Wheway, the
previous owners of Champneys, have
introduced the same successful
formula to the Sanctuary. This is the
health and beauty spa for women.
A peaceful haven of tropical and
spacious surroundings. Feel relaxed
in the pools, sauna and steam rooms.
The body treatments, facials,
massage, aromatherapy, reflexology,
hydrotherapy leave you completely
revitalised. Ask for the 'Ultimate
Escape Day' when booking.

St James' Health And Sauna Club
7-9 St James's Street SW1
Tel: 0171 930 5870
Open: Mon-Fri 9.30-10pm;
Sat 10am-9pm and Sun 12noon-9pm.
Quite close to Piccadilly you will find
this well-respected health club with a
gym, plunge pool, solarium. Sauna
and one hour massage £40.

The Tanning Shop
4 Campden Hill Road Kensington W8
Tel: 0171 938 1932
Open: Mon-Sat 8am-8pm;
Sun 10am-6pm
Approximately 35 branches through -
out London each with a stand-up
sunroom and a toning machine. £5 for
6 minutes, £12 for 15 minutes.The
best value for money is the one hour
course at £50, or the two hour course,
costing £70.

Health Farms

First they starve you, then they strip you, pummel you, casserole you in a cabinet, plunge your medium-rare body into icy water, and rub salt into your par boiled skin. It sounds like a torture, but you feel marvellous. And, as a solicitous attendant wraps you in a warm, fluffy towel and eases you into a reclining chair with the morning papers and a glass of lemon juice, somehow you can't help feeling that this is the good life.

That is why more and more people are flocking to this uniquely British institution the health farm.
There are a half dozen in the big league: Champneys, Ragdale Hall, Inglewood, Forest Mere. Grayshott, Cedar Falls. Most approximately within an hour's drive from London, they offer a geographical choice but do not differ markedly in treatment or amenities.
Although many of the clientele come from the top echelons of society, even royalty, there are others of more slender means, people who realise they've spent time and money lavishly servicing their cars, while neglecting that infinitely more delicate machine - their own body.

Diplomats and business leaders, often suffering from a surfeit of weight, worry and stress, figure strongly in the visitors books. So, too, do show business personalities

and professional men with a nexus of tensions induced by a competitive work environment. But the vast majority of clients are women in search of rest as much as youth and beauty, escaping from the double burden of job and home.

One health farm has as its motto: "Adding years to your life; taking years off your face and figure." All aim to achieve this by their unique service of solicitude and care, segregated from the stresses, strains, noise and vexations of day-to-day living. Smoking is discouraged. Drinking is prohibited. The body is cleansed by diet. The mind is relaxed. Nerves are untautened. Surplus weight evaporates along with cares.

Most of the health farms have superb facilities, dedicated staff, and a philosophy of total natural health. Basically they provide a combination of corrective eating which generally means progressing from fasting via grapefruit and lemon juice to whole - some home-made yoghurt and home-grown unadulterated fresh salads, fruit and vegetables and lean fish and meat.

Typically, the process starts with a thorough physical checkup, when a consultant doctor, osteopath or matron gives you an intensive consultation, weighing and measuring and taking your blood pressure. Diet is then mapped out, and specialist therapy prescribed. Treatment includes massage, saunas, steam-baths, wax baths, hot mud, underwater massage, and various forms of alternate stimulation and relaxation with complex apparatus.

Where prescribed, there is physiotherapy, osteopathy, electrotherapy, hydrotherapy, remedial gymnastics, and other techniques of conventional and fringe medicine.

For some patients, rest is the treatment, with classes in yoga and meditation. Others are prescribed as much activity as possible, with dancing, bridge, backgammon, chess, scrabble, billiards, table tennis, croquet and non-competitive handicrafts like pottery, painting, and flower-arranging. And for the athletic there is swimming, PT, jogging, tennis, riding and golf. Most clients measure success in terms of weight loss.The ambience is one of blissfully serene tranquillity. Children and pets are banned. There is an extremely high ratio of staff to guest (1.5 to one) and everyone is trained to please. It is unashamedly luxurious, pampering away your aches and anxieties in return for a certain amount of self-discipline and self-denial. This is a typical day's routine prescribed.

Orange juice in bed at 7.15 am. Matron visits room at 7.30 to discuss progress and day's schedule. At 9.30, report for a warm shower, then go in the sauna. The sauna session is intermittently interrupted for an impulse shower with alternating hot and cold needle jets to encourage perspiration in the sauna.

Next, after a rest, I am collected by a blonde masseuse whose professional skill matches her good looks. I never before realised a massage could be so relaxing.I have a G5. That's a vibrating machine that tones the skin and surface tissues, and it's followed by infra red heat to relieve backache,

After a crisp salad lunch, and a break to digest it, I walk through the gardens. Afternoon tea is much appreciated. So is an introductory meditation session demonstrating the art of relaxation.

Like a game of snakes and ladders, a stay at a health farm is a matter of gains arid losses. The brochures promise that you acquire health, vitality and vigour, while losing pounds in weight and inches in shape. Large claims, but I can vouch for it. The trouble is that the feeling of well-being generates a lusty appetite for the very self-indulgences that will necessitate taking the cure again in a few months, That, surely, is the secret of their success.

Please Note

This is a brief list of some of the most popular and more accessible health farms within easy reach of London. Prices change and special promotions become available from time to time. The prices quoted are accurate at the time of going to press

Ragdale Hall

Near Melton Mowbray Leicestershire
Telephone: 01664 434831
By rail: St. Pancras to Leicester
By road : M1 to junction 21A to A46
The airy and calming Ragdale Hall is the ideal place to relax. Special offers available, including a Ragdale Day costing from £75. Two people sharing £84 per person per night, which includes all meals and several treatments.

Springs Hydro

Packington, Leicstershire
Telephone: 01530 273873
By rail: St Pancras to Loughborough;
By road: M42

Promotions usually available - especially "Bring a Friend Free" and Top to Toe Days. Average cost for a couple, £199 per person for 2 nights accommodation, treatments and meals.

Henlow Grange

Henlow Bedfordshire
Telephone: 01462 811111
By rail Kings Cross to Arlesey station;
By road: A1 Motorway
Mother and Daughter special promotion. Weight loss programme. Weekend £500 includes two nights, all meals and use of the facilities, plus free treatments. One-day specials cost £100 and that includes all treatments.

Inglewood

Kintbury Berkshire
Telephone: 01488 685111
By rail: Paddington to Kintbury;
By road: M4 Junction 13
15% discount single room for 3 nights. Day packages start at £70 and include lunch and use of all facilities.

Ragdale Hall: set in the peaceful surroundings of Leicestershire countryside

The completely revised edition of Night Out in London
will be on sale in December 1999
and will be available from all four and five-star hotel-shops
and selected branches of the
book and magazine retail trade.
Please photocopy and return the order form below

ORDER FORM

Please supply me with _____ copies of Night Out in London
at £4.99 per copy.

☐ I enclose a cheque for £_____ made payable to:
Niche Publications.

☐ I enclose my order on company letterhead,
please invoice me (UK registered companies only)

☐ Please debit my credit Access/Visa card account

Card number ☐☐☐☐☐☐☐☐☐☐☐☐☐☐☐☐☐☐

expiry date_____

Name as shown on the card _____

Signature_____

Please send an advance copy of your next edition to:

Name _____

Address _____

_____

_____ Post code_____

Please return this order form to: Niche Publications P.O. Box 20988
31 London Street London W2 3GX.

Wine and Cocktail Bars

"Boozers are for losers! So sneer the wine snobs". Wine Bars are for whiners!" is the traditionalists riposte. Fortunately they don't say what cocktail bars are for. The fact of the matter is that the fag-ash four ale bar has become a misnomer. A dying brewed.

Remember the days when a request for a glass of wine produced querulously raised eyebrows and, after as long search, a near empty bottle of Entre Deux Mers?" Is it dry?" One queried. "Not very. It's just come out that bucket of tepid water.. "But then the Innkeeper stared at the label and added reassuringly. "Oh, it's a good 'un this. Entre Deux Mers. Between two Mothers." How things have changed!

Shampers, the all day favourite in West Soho near Carnaby Street, has no less than seventeen varieties of Grand Marque bubbly and a selection of the finest wines from around the world -over two hundred at the last stocktaking! Even Brown Ale is becoming a thing of the past as glamourous new bars open across the Capital selling sophisticated alternatives like Leffe Blonde and Hoegaarden.

BBB (Beach Blanket Babylon) in the very trendy Notting Hill area is open daily between 5.30pm-11pm This is a very stylish bar with fabulous lip-shaped couches, carved stone fireplaces and ecclesiastical statues. Most evenings you will find the place buzzing with a young, arty sophisticated crowd. The restaurant has a modern international menu.

All Bar One : A very popular bar for the twentysomethings

Cocktail/Wine Bars

192
192 Kensington Park Road W11
Tel: 0171 229 4481
Open: Mon-Sun 12.30pm-3.15pm and
6.30pm-11.30pm
A popular meeting place for pop
stars, writers and a good general mix
of locals. Getting a table can be quite
difficult if you choose to eat in the
downstairs restaurant, where the
food is classic but the service can be
erratic.

All Bar One
36-38 Dean Street Soho W1
Tel: 0171 287 4641
Mon-Sun 11.30am-11pm
This is one of the most popular bars
in this comparatively new chain to
hit our established drinking areas.
Lively twentysomethings from local
advertising agencies and film
companies make up the crowd.

Bar Solona
17 Old Compton Street Soho W1
Tel: 0171 287 9932
Mon-Fri 5.30pm-2am Sat 7pm-2am
Fun Mexican basement bar with loud
Spanish music and a lively interior -
Tex-Mex style with tiled floors, bright
colours and cacti-painted on the walls.

BBB (Beach Blanket Babylon)
45 Ledbury Road, W11
Tel: 0171 229 2907
Open: daily 5.30pm-11pm
A very stylish bar with fabulous
lip-shaped couches, carved stone
fireplaces and ecclesiastical statues.
Always buzzing with a young, arty
sophisticated crowd. The restaurant
has a modern international menu.

Trader Vic's Hilton Hotel Park Lane: Where
the cocktails can be quite deceptive

The Buzz Bar
32 Panton Street Haymarket SW1
Tel: 0171 839 8939
Happy hour Tue and Thurs.
50's and 60's memorabilia that
include a motor bike. The Buzz Bar is
a dynamic bar/night club with
waitresses in swimsuits and waiters
in cycling shorts. Various dancing
areas help you to groove to the latest
dance music. The ideal venue for the
young - and the young at heart.

Café Royal Cocktail Bar
68 Regent Street Picadilly Circus W1
Tel: 0171 437 9090
Open to 11pm; Sun to 6pm
What the famous Café Royal Cocktail
lacks in its name it makes up for in
its ingredients: whisky, mandarin,
napoleon and green chartreuse, with
lime, tangerine juice and champagne.

ABSOLUT PROFILE.

WHICHEVER WAY YOU LOOK AT IT, THERE IS NO PURER VODKA. ENJOY NEAT, ICE-COLD.

Cheers

72 Regent Street Piccadilly Circus W1.
Tel: 0171 494 3322.
Cheers has something for everyone. It's open for coffee from 11am, over-looking Regent Street. Lunch is available from 12noon and there is a resting bar for shoppers all day. Happy hour cocktails are available from 5pm and there are pre and post-cinema and theatre menus on offer. Two large TV screens show sport all day and the in-house DJ plays from 11pm until 3am. All this, just one minute's walk from Piccadilly Circus.

Cork and Bottle

44 Cranbourn Street WC2
Tel: 0171 734 6592
Open: Mon-Sat 11am-12pm
Sun 12am-10.30pm
A tiny entrance conceals one of the best wine bars in the West End. Award-winning, it attracts faithful bands of connoisseurs who like the Provençal-style food and value-for-money wines.

The Doghouse

187 Wardour Street Soho W1
Tel: 0171 434 2116
Open: Mon-Sat 5pm-11pm
The almost unnoticeable doorway leads down into this popular lively designer bar, quirkily decorated in a riot of reds, oranges and blues. Renowned for its variety of chilled vodka shots. If you like your music loud and funky- this is the place for you.

Finos wine cellar

123 Mount Street W1
Tel: 0171 491 1640
Open: Mon-Sat 12noon-3pm;
Mon-Fri 6pm-11pm
In this underground wine bar you can hide away from the entire world. It has one long bar with a function room, The Board Room, at the back. Then it has some of the coziest caves to be found in London. The bar is family run and the owners make fresh crisps on the premises which are given away free of charge.

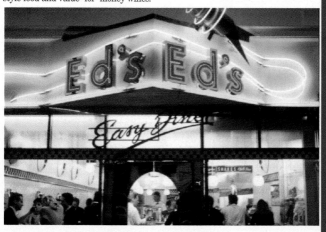

Harvey's
46 Gloucester Terrace W2
Tel: 0171 402 1100
Open Mon-Sat 12noon -midnight
This family run intimate little bar in Paddington seems to attract all the local eccentrics. The crowd are generally more interesting that the the entire fly-on-the-wall television series 'Paddington Green' - which focused on a transsexual, a wig maker and a homosexual estate agent. Off - the -wall David Zubedi has even gone so far as to form a 'Paddingtonian Society.' To qualify for membership you have to be noticed by a existing member doing something, or saying something out of the ordinary. The panel decides.

Henry's Cafe Bars
80 Piccadilly W1 (Near Green Park)
Tel: 0171 491 2544
Open: Mon-Fri 8am-11pm;
Sat 9am-11pm; Sun 10am-10.30pm
Endell Street WC2 and
346 High Street Kensington W14
These restaurants and bars are becoming synonymous with great food and drink, intoxicating atmosphere and quality of service. Well worth a visit.

Jimmies Wine Bar
18 Kensington Church Street W8
Tel: 0171 937 9988
Open for lunch and dinner
Mon-Sat 12noon-1am
Live music Tue-Sat 9.30pm-1am
Well-established basement wine bar

The elegant surroundings of the **Cafe Royal** in Regent Street

with live music ranging from Rock, Soul, Jazz and Calypso (depending on the night) and a full menu including pastas, steaks and fish. Spirits are also available as well as a very comprehensive wine list.

Janet's Bar
208 Fulham Road SW10
Tel: 0171 795 0111
Open: Mon-Sat 12noon-11pm;
Sun 12noon-10.30pm
Janet and David Evans the City lawyers whose dream it was to have their own bar. The result is a pink and white sugar-candy-looking facade with pink wicker chairs on the pavement. Inside, a marble-topped bar fills almost half the room, and the stark white walls, pink accessories and numourous fitness activities collages adorn the bar. Camp is one word to describe it; adventurous and kitsch are others. Undeniably self - indulgent is what it actually is, but nevertheless worth a visit.

Julie's
137 Portland Road W11
Tel: 0171 727 7985
Two bars, each having its own
separate character. Downstairs is
functional with wood furniture and
mirrors, upstairs is more informal. A
long time favourite with Sloanes,
Yuppies and a generous offering of
used-car salesmen in Armani suits.

Kettner's Champagne Bar
29 Romilly Street W1
Tel: 0171 437 6437
Open: Daily to 12am
Fashionable bar with an
antiquarian elegance that makes it
very warm and snug, and a list of
over seventy varieties of champagne.
One of the best in Soho.

Shampers
4 Kingly Street West Soho W1
Tel: 0171 437 1692
Open: Mon-Sat 11am-11pm
Close to Carnaby Street you will find
a haven for lovers of bubbly, offering
17 different Grand Marque labels.
The actual wine bar itself is on the
ground floor; a brasserie occupies the
basement. Altogether, the place offers
an extraordinary number of wines -
over 200 at the last count - so you
need never be at a loss for something
new to try.

Smollensky's Balloon
1 Dover Street W1
Tel: 0171 491 1199
Open: Mon-Sat-11am-11pm;
Sun12noon-10.30pm
Bar and restaurant with a wood and
chrome look and video screens above
the bar. Try their Bourbon Street
Breeze cocktail.

Smollensky's Balloon Dover Street W1

Tearoom des Artistes
697 Wandsworth Road SW8
Tel: 0171 652 6526
Open: Mon-Fri 5pm-1am
Sat and Sun 12.30 pm-1am
Don't be deceived by the name;
although tea is served, this is a
lively and quite bohemian bar and
restaurant with plenty of outdoor
seating in the garden or patio with
jazz on Sundays.

TGI Friday's
6 Bedford St Covent Garden WC2
Tel: 0171 379 0585
Open: Mon-Sun 11am-11pm
One of the few bars that actually
creates a good family atmosphere
and also manages to attract the
'trendy/ groovy' singles crowd. Most
of these 'middle American'
restaurants/ bars are in prominent
locations, and for your nearest one
phone the above number.

Trader Vic's
The Hilton Hotel Park Lane W1
Tel: 0171 208 4113
Open: Mon-Sat 5pm.-12.45am;
Sun 5pm-10.30pm
The original cocktail theme bar,
situated below the Hilton Hotel,
with enormous bowls of pink punch,
South Pacific decor and waitresses in
appropriate attire.

Titanic
81 Brewer Street
Piccadilly Circus W1
Tel: 0171 437 1912
Open Mon-Sat 12noon-2.30am; Sun
5.30pm-10.30pm
"The future is affordable glamour
with good honest food." the words of
mercurial Marco Pierre White, one of
the most exciting chefs in London.
He seems to enjoy creating genuinely
elegant environments and his
penchant for glitter balls extends
from the Mirabelle to his new
Titanic. Both attract the style set.

Theatre

Time after time, the West End has defied the pessimists and bounced up from its sick-bed with renewed vigour. Shows may open and close within weeks or take up seemingly permanent residence, but the London theatre endures gallantly through both feast and famine – surviving flop and box office blockbuster alike.

Although the Society of London Theatre includes both subsidised flagships (the Royal National on the South Bank of the Thames and the Barbican's RSC) the main core of activity is concentrated in the heart of London along inter-connecting thoroughfares.

An energetic walker can start at the outlying Whitehall Theatre on the fringes of Trafalgar Square and amble up the Strand, past the Adelphi, Vaudeville, Strand and Aldwych theatres with a sidelong glance at the Theatre Royal, Drury Lane. This theatre, rather confusingly, is not actually in Drury Lane – that honour goes to the New London where Cats has been purring since 1981.
The main artery is Shaftesbury Avenue, where four theatres stand in blocks of two: the Lyric cheek by jowl with the Apollo, the Gielgud (formerly the Globe) side by side with the Queen's. At the end of the Avenue stands the Palace, home of Les Miserables and a sentinel over Cambridge Circus which divides another principal street of theatreland Charing Cross Road. North of Cambridge Circus stands the Phoenix. In recent years this was reckoned to be London's voodoo theatre after a succession of flops.
To the South is the Garrick and Wyndham's which stands back-to-back with the Albery in St Martin's Lane, even sharing a stage door.

Mamma Mia !. here they go again.

A few steps away from the Albery is the Duke of York's and the royal theatre is maintained in the Prince of Wales, just off Leicester Square and the Prince Edward in Old Compton Street now playing host to Mamma Mia.

London's fifty odd theatres prefer to huddle close together for security. The little Ambassadors was the original host and home for so many years to The Mousetrap, now in its 49th year, which moved all of a few feet to the neighbouring St.Martin's. The ornate splendours of the Theatre Royal, Haymarket, where glittering packages of stars are faced by the imposing facade of Her Majesty's by snaking queues of hopefuls still waiting for returns to Phantom Of The Opera. Some have been camping on the pavements, it seems, since the show opened in October 1986. There are also quirky, rather far flung oddities.

There is a little colony of theatres in Victoria. The first sight which one glimpses on emerging from the station is the Victoria Palace Theatre. At the neighbouring Apollo Victoria, Starlight Express shows no sign of going off the rails.

Around twelve million people paid admission to the London theatres last year, but this does not include the thousands who attended shows at the theatres on the edge of Central London and the large number of enthusiasts who prefer to visit all the various venues known for convenience as 'The Fringe'.

The three stages of the Royal National, the Lyttelton, Olivier and Cottesloe and the two Royal Shakespeare Company (RSC) venues, the Barbican and the Pit, operate a repertory system and can play up to three or four different productions a week. Although both complexes drew flak from die-hard traditionalists in the early years the foyers, numerous bars and buffets combined with the generally relaxed atmosphere are in stark contrast to the bedlam which is the average West End theatre bar during the interval rush.

Forecasting trends in the London theatre is an entertaining but valueless way to pass the time but let's have a shot. It seems likely that the taste for spectacular musicals of the kind like Les Miserables, Phantom of the Opera, and Chicago will continue to grow but the encouraging return to more serious, testing drama will be maintained.

Successes from all parts of Broadway will continue to be presented in the hope of striking lucky twice and the subsidised sector will prove increasingly useful in sharing the burden of costs with West End producers. The search for the sure-fire hit will be pursued as eagerly as ever.

People with disabilities

A free information and advice service to the arts, is available for people with disabilities by phoning 0171 388 2227

Booking seats

Seats may be booked directly at the theatre box office, making payment by cash, cheque or credit card (normally between 10am and 8pm Monday to Friday). Booking in person allows the seats to be chosen from the full- size seating plan, and ensures more choice, although if the show is very popular you may be disappointed to find it sold out - which it probably isn't, but in order to book seats you will have to go to a ticket agent.

If you have plenty of time you could arrive about an hour before 'curtain up' and queue for standby tickets. Bookings will be taken by telephone through the box office.
Theatres usually require telephone bookings to be made at least three days in advance and payment is made by credit card. Tickets will be held at the box office for collection, but bookings not paid on time will go on standby sale one hour before curtain-up. Theatre ticket agencies abound in central London, and are usually the only source of booking for "hot ticket" shows, as theatres assign up to 30% of tickets to them. Agencies charge a service fee of 15-20%, but accept telephone and telephone credit card bookings and many will deliver tickets within central London.

The Phantom of the Opera: Still one of the hot tickets in town

Half price tickets

The Society of London Theatres operates a ticket booth in Leicester Square, where tickets for most West End productions are available on the day of the show. All tickets are half - price, plus a 75pence service charge and payment is by cash with four tickets only to each customer. The booth is open from midday for matinees and between 12.30-6.30pm for evening performances. All you have to do is turn up in person and wait in a queue for tickets to be released and sold for the night's performances. For information on shows, including daily seat availability telephone the theatre box office, or contact: The Society of London Theatres: 0171 836 0971

Chicago
Adelphi Strand WC2
Tel: 0171 344 0055
Performance Length approx. 2h50m
Recast and revivified, Kander and Ebb's
Chicago, with its alluring songs and
acerbic lyrics. Two Twenties gals have
murdered their men and are scheming to
get out of jail.The dancing and the
production itself remain top notch and
can only be seen as a triumph of dapper
decadence.

Starlight Express
Apollo Victoria, SW1
Tel: 0171 828 8665
Performance Length approx. 2h30
Andrew Lloyd-Webber's revamped
musical extravaganza with the entire
cast of 40 on roller blades. The plot,
involving a competition to find the fastest
engine on the American railroad, goes
almost unnoticed amid the special effects
under Trevor Nunn's wonderful
direction.

Beauty and The Beast
Dominion Tottenham Court Road W1
Tel: 0171 656 1888 (Ends December 1999)
Mon-Sat 19.30; mats Wed, Sat 14.30;
Performance length 2h40
Music by Alan Menken, lyrics by Howard
Ashman and Tim Rice. By far the most
expensive musical staged in London,
based on the Disney blockbuster
from the traditional fairy
tale. This all year round
pantomime will run
happily ever after.

The Woman in Black
Fortune Russell Street WC2
Tel: 0171 836 2238
Performance length approx. 1h50
Isn't it wonderful to find a thriller tha
thrills ? If it's the hair standing on en
and the tingles down the spine you se
this long-running ghost story adapte
Stephen Mallatratt from the famous
by Susan Hill will haunt you forever..

An Inspector Calls
Garrick 2 Charing Cross Road WC2
Tel:0171 494 5085
Performance length 1h50
The Royal National's acclaimed
production of J.B. Priestley's classic
thriller has now won 19 major awar
One of the most exciting revivals of
decade enhanced by Stephen Daldry
brilliant direction and Ian MacNeil's
expressionistic design which brings
house down in an unforgettable cou
theatre. Call the Inspector now.

Shows can change at short notice.
Check with the box office before
planning your
evening

"A SHOWSTOPPING SHOW, A GAUDY, GLORIOUS, GLITTERING HIT... A KILLER THRILLER"
SUNDAY TIMES

CHICAGO

The Phantom of the Opera
Her Majesty's Haymarket SW1
Tel: 0171 494 5400
Performance Length: 2h30
Andrew Lloyd Webber's romantic musical, based on Gaston Leroux's gothic novel of life beneath the haunted stage of the Paris Opera, has been a sell-out for a generation and is as spell-binding now as when it first opened. Watch out for the chandelier!

Saturday Night Fever
London Palladium Argyll Street W1
Tel: 0171 494 5020
Performance length approx. 2h.40
The very popular Seventies disco film that launched the career of John Travolta as an international star, has adapted very well to a singing dancing musical on stage. All the big 'Bee Gee' hits from the movie adds up to being a great night out if you want to revel in nostalgia.

Cats
New London Drury Lane WC2
Tel: 0171 405 0072
Performance length approx. 2h45
Andrew Lloyd Webber's international award-winning moggie musical is now in it's 16th year, making it by far the longest running musical on Broadway and in London. Directed by Trevor Nunn, choreographed by Gillian Lynne and based on T.S. Elliot's Old Possum's Book of Practical Cats, it's a feline fantasy in which the fur really flies.

Les Miserables
Palace Shaftesbury Avenue W1
Tel: 0171 434 0909
Performance length approx.
The musical version of Victor Hugo's masterpiece about love and courage during the revolutionary struggles of19th century France, has stormed the barricades all over the world. Now in it's 14th overwhelming year.

West End Theatres

ADELPHI Strand WC2	0171 379 8884
ALBERY St Martin's Lane WC2	0171 369 1730
ALDYWCH Aldwych WC2	0171 416 6003
AMBASSADORS West Street WC2	0171 836 6111
APOLLO Shaftesbury Avenue W1	0171 494 5070
APOLLO VICTORIA SW1	0171 828 8665
ARTS Great Newport Street WC2	0171 836 2132
BARBICAN Silk Street EC2	0171 638 8891
CAMBRIDGE Earlham Street SE1	0171 494 5080
COMEDY Panton Street SW1	0171 369 1731
CRITERION Piccadilly SW1	0171 839 4488
DOMINION Tottemham Court Rd	0171 416 6060
DRURY LANE Drury Lane WC2	0171 494 5100
DUKE OF YORK'S St Martin's Lane WC2	0171 836 5122
FORTUNE Russell Street WC2	0171 836 2238
GARRICK Charing Cross Road WC2	0171 494 5085
GIELGUD Shaftesbury Avenue W1	0171 494 5065
HAYMARKET Haymarket SW1	0171 930 8800
HER MAJESTY'S Haymarket SW1	0171 494 5400
LONDON PALLADIUM Argyll Street W1	0171 494 5020
LYRIC Shaftesbury Avenue W1	0171 494 5045
MERMAID Puddle Dock EC4	0171 236 2211
NATIONAL THEATRE South Bank SE1	0171 928 2252
NEW LONDON Drury Lane WC2	0171 405 0072
OLD VIC Waterloo Road SE1	0171 928 7616
PALACE Shaftesbury Avenue W1	0171 434 0909
PHOENIX Charing Cross Road WC2	0171 369 1733
PICCADILLY Denman Street W1	0171 369 1734
EDWARD Old Compton Street W1	0171 734 8951
PRINCE OF WALES Coventry Street W1	0171 839 5987
QUEENS Shaftesbury Avenue W1	0171 494 5040
ST MARTIN'S West Street WC2	0171 836 1443
SAVOY Strand WC2	0171 836 8888
SHAKESPEARES GLOBE Bear Gardens SE1	0171 928 7710
SHAFTESBURY Shaftesbury Avenue WC2	0171 379 5399
STRAND Aldwych WC2	0171 930 8800
VAUDEVILLE Strand WC2	0171 836 9987
VICTORIA PALACE Victoria SW1	0171 834 1317
WHITEHALL Whitehall SW1	0171 369 1735
WYNDHAMS Charing Cross Road WC2	0171 369 1746
YOUNG VIC 66 The Cut SE1	0171 928 6363

Blood Brothers
Phoenix Charing Cross Road WC2
Tel: 0171 369 1733
Performance length approx. 2h45
Willy Russell's long-running, award laden musical features the lives of Liverpudlian twins, separated at birth, whose paths are destined to cross again. Memorable songs, passion, melodrama on a grand scale and not a dry eye in the house.

Mamma Mia
Prince Edward Shaftesbury Ave W1
Tel: 0171 447 5400
Performance length approx. 2h45
This is a story knitted together about romance and not the 'Abba Story -'. although it has twenty seven of their popular songs The action takes place on a Greek Island where a mother is about to marry off her daughter.
An absolute must for devotees of the group and with songs like 'Thank You For The Music' and of course 'Mamma Mia', I can see it being one of the hot tickets for a long time to come.

West Side Story
Prince of Wales Coventry Street W1
Tel: 0171 839 5987
Performance length approx. 2h40
Forty years on and still as popular as ever. Leonard Bernstein's score, with its feverish currents of sexual energy and adolescent gangland aggression, still remains one of the most exciting musicals to hit the West End stage.

The Mousetrap
St Martin's West Street WC2
Tel: 0171 836 1443
Performance length approx. 2h15
An assorted bunch of typical Agatha Christie characters are snowed up in a lonely country house and there's a murderer about... This classic comedy-thriller packs them in nightly by the coach-load. Its destined to run forever now that it has survived both the writer and forty seven years in the West End.

A dramatic scene from Les Miserables

Popular Cinemas

ABC PANTON STREET .SW1	0171 930 0631
ABC Piccadilly W1	0171 437 3561
ABC SHAFTESBURY AVENUE W1	0171 836 6279
ABC SWISS CENTRE W1	0171 439 4470
ABC TOTTENHAM COURT ROAD W1	0171-636 6148
BARBICAN	0171 382 7000
CHELSEA KING'S ROAD SW3	0171 351 3742
CORONET Notting Hill Gate. W11	0171 727 6705
CURZON MAYFAIR Curzon Street W1	0171-369 1720
CURZON SOHO Shaftesbury Avenue W1	0171-439 4805
GATE Notting Hill Gate W11	0171 727 4043
MINEMA KNIGHTSBRIDGE SW1	0171 369 1723
METRO 11 Rupert Street W1	0171 437 0757
ODEON KENSINGTON Kensington High Street W8	0870 5050
ODEON LEICESTER SQUARE W1	0870 5050
ODEON MARBLE ARCH W2	0870 5050
ODEON MAZZANINE Leicester Square W1	0870 5050
ODEON WEST END Leicester Square W1	0870 5050
PRINCE CHARLES Leicester Place WC2	0171-437 8181
RENOIR Brunswick Square WC1	0171 837 8402
SCREEN ON BAKER STREET W1	0171 935 2772
SCREEN ON THE GREEN Islington Green N1	0171 226 3520
SCREEN ON THE HILL 230 Haverstock Hill NW3	0171 435 3366
TRICYCLE CINEMA Kilburn High Road NW6	0171 435 3366
UCI PLAZA Piccadilly Circus W1	0990 888990
UCI WHITELEYS Queensway W2	0171 792 3332
VIRGIN CHELSEA Kings Road SW3	0870 9007
VIRGIN FULHAM Fulham Road SW6	0870 907 0711
VIRGIN Hammersmith W6	0870 907 0718

Eating Out in Theatreland

The Criterion
Piccadilly Circus SW1
Tel: 0171 925 0909
Open:Mon-Sat 12noon-11pm.
Sun 12-noon10.30pm
A Piccadilly landmark restored to previous grandeur with details like a gold mosaic ceiling, candelabras and recessed arches. Italian/American menu.

Joy King Lau
3 Leicester Street WC2
Tel: 0171 437 1132
Open:daily 12 noon-11.30pm
A long established, tastefully decorated Chinese restaurant in the heart of theatreland. The seafood and service are both excellent.

Rowleys
113 Jermyn Street, SW1
Tel: 0171 930 2707
Open: Noon-3pm & 6pm-11.30pm
Traditional English restaurant, located in a historical building in this classy area. It still manages to retain a relaxed atmosphere despite the formal surroundings.

Simpson-in-the-Strand
100 The Strand WC2
Tel: 0171 836 9112
Mon-Sat 12noon -2pm and 6pm-9pm
Another fine restaurant offering the best of traditional English cuisine, from their highly recommended roast beef to 'bangers and mash'.

Amalfi
29 Old Compton Street W1
Tel: 0171 437 7284
Open Mon-Sun 9am-10pm
A restaurant and cake shop in Soho offering traditional Italian cuisine that is excellent value for money. Their table-tops are covered by painted tiles depicting the coastal scenes of Amalfi. The Sorana di Pollo Sarlinesi is great.

Arirang
31-32 Poland Street W1
Tel: 0171 437 6633
Open: Mon-Sat 12noon-3pm; 6pm - 11pm. Closed Sun.
A small, pleasant, family- run, and unpretentious restaurant serving traditional Dorian cuisine. Popular with local and visiting Koreans. Special dishes include bulgogi, kal bee jim, bul kat bee, yuk kew, bintatok, kim & kim-chee pokum. There is han jeong sik for the family.

Bentley's Oyster Bar
11/15 Swallow Street W1
Tel: 0171 734 4756
Restaurant/ Oyster bar /Brasserie
Open Mon-Sat 11am-11pm;Cabin Bar: 12Noon-11pm
This delightfully old-fashioned fish restaurant established in the middle of the first World war. Formal dining upstairs with booth seating. and ground level oyster bar and set price theatre menu.

Beotys
79 St Martin's Lane WC2
Tel: 0171 836 8768
Mon-Sat 12.15- 3 and 5.30-11.30
Comfortable family-run restaurant with long-serving staff who offer a friendly welcome. 'Franco-Greek' cuisine with Greek-Cypriot specialities.

Bertorellis
44a Floral Street WC2
Tel: 0171 836 1868
Open: Mon-Sun 6pm-11.30pm
Popular and stylish modern Italian restaurant and café which is situated next to the Royal Opera House. Serves traditional favourites and new Italian dishes.

Flounders
19-21 Tavistock Street WC2
Tel: 0171 836 3925
Open: Mon-Sat 12noon-2.30pm; Mon-Fri and 5.30pm-midnight
A charming little theatreland restaurant specialising in fish dishes. A special pre-theatre menu represents good value for money.

Hamiltons Brasserie
Whitcomb Street Leicester Sq.WC2
Tel: 0171 839 5151
Open: Mon-Sat Noon-Midnight
Sun 8am-10.30pm
Relaxed hotel brasserie with good value, set-price menus and daily specials, as well as à la carte.

Manzis

1-2 Leicester Street WC2
Tel: 0171 734 0224
Open: Lunch: Mon-Sat 12-2.30pm;
Dinner: 5.30-11.30pm
One of London's oldest Italian seafood
restaurants and close to all theatres.
Family run and splendidly decorated.
The range of dishes on offer is
generous and extensive.

Mon Plaisir

21 Monmouth Street WC2
Tel: 0171 836 7243
Open: Mon-Sat 12noon-2.15;
6pm-11.15 pm Closed Sunday.
The oldest French family-run eatery
in the heart of the West End. Traditional cuisine in intimate atmosphere.
Ideally located for theatre-goers.
They serve North Indian authentic
cuisine and take great pride in their
quality of food and service.

The Red Fort

77 Dean Street W1
Tel: 0171 437 2525
Open daily : Noon-2.45pm; 6pm-11pm
A far cry from the vast majority of
Indian restaurants. The modern
cuisine also includes Bangladeshi
dishes.

Spaghetti House

24 Cranbourn Street, W1
Tel: 0171 836 8168
Open: Mon-Sat Noon-11pm
Sun 5.30pm-10.30pm
All the restaurants in the Spaghetti
House chain are close to the focal
points of London, and this one is ideal
for the theatre and West End cinemas.
They specialise in fresh pasta made
daily.

The Criterion- The perfect place to eat either before of after the theatre

Artsline

54 Chalton Street London NW1 1HS
Tel: 0171 388 2227
E-mail: artsline@dircon.co.uk
web:http//www.dircon.co.uk artsline
Open daily 9.30am-5.30pm
Artsline is London's information and
advice service on access to the arts &
entertainment for all disabled people.

Backstage Tours

at Theatre Royal Drury Lane WC2
Tel: 0171 240 5357
Mon,Tue,Thu, Fri 11am-1pm and
5.30pm; Wed and Sat 11am-12.30pm;
Sun 12noon-2pm and 3.30pm
One of London's oldest and finest
Theatres offers dramatic tours of its
historic backstage at a cost of £4 per
person. Quite an enlightening, and
haunting experience.

The Celebrity Bulletin

93/97 Regent Street W1
Tel: 0171 439 9840
If you want to subscribe to the
Celebrity Bulletin it will cost you £60
a month. The information provided
will give you the name of a public
relations contact or reveal where the
visiting celebrity may be contacted.

Theatre Museum

Russell Street Covent Garden WC2
Tel: 0171 836 7891
Open Tue-Sun between 11am-7pm
The Theatre Museum houses
permanent displays and special
exhibitions drawn from the Museum's
wonderful collections, with a souvenir
shop and box office for West End
Shows. A study room is available for
research by prior arrangement.

Museum Of The Moving Image

South Bank Waterloo SE1
Open daily 10am- 6pm
Tel: 0171 401 2636
The magical world of film and
television comes to life before your
very eyes. Here you're the star. You
can fly like Superman, become a news
reader or audition for a Hollywood
screen role; watch hundreds of film
and TV clips, and interact with the
cast of actor guides.

Television Audience

If you would like to join a studio
audience and watch your favourite
T.V. or radio show being recorded,
write to the following contacts and
enclose a stamped, self- addressed
envelope with your choice. Most
independent filmmakers have
different procedures, and you would
need to contact them directly:-

BBC Radio Ticket Unit W1A 4WW

Tel: 0171 765 5243 or 0171 765 5858

BBC Television Unit

Room 301 Design Building
Television Centre W12 7RJ
Tel: 0181 576 1227
For recorded information service.

London Weekend Television

The Audience Unit Television Centre
Upper Ground London SE1
Tel: 0171 261 3447

Comedy

If its laughter you're after you're on in London! At the last count there were almost 150 venues across the Capital offering embryonic entertainers to rival Sir Bob Hope, Charlie Chaplin, Peter Sellers, Eddie lzzard, Harry Enfield, French and Saunders, Ben Elton and so many others too numourous to mention. The tradition goes on!

The main contenders to look out for are Boothby Graffoe, Tina C. Rhinestone Cowgirl a lovely Tranny who sings Country & Western song send-ups. Her new album is entitled 'Complete and Utter Country'. For those who don't know (do try to keep up at the back!) Trannies are transsexuals/transvestites, following in the tradition of music hall stars Mrs Shufflewick and Old Mother Riley and every other Dame in Pantomime since time immoral.

Omid Djalili was Britains first Iranian stand-up comic, but he has a rival, believe it or not, in Shappi Khorsandi who is hard on his heels in the try-out circuit.
The 'comedy club' owes its existence to the 'Alternative Comedian'. This creature was spawned in the eighties in a dingy theatre which formed part of the Raymond Revuebar in Soho. It was called aptly enough the

'Comic Strip'. Next door, nubile dancers were baring their torsos while on this stage febrile comics were paring themselves down to their funny bones. The audiences loved the irreverent and anarchic personas of these mainly young performers.

This is where the comic talents of our finest comedians today were discovered . They were dubbed 'Alternative' by a journalist, meaning 'different to the usual clapped out stuff' or perhaps just 'funny'. Unknowns then, nowadays they seem to 'Alternate' with each other every other night on B.B.C and I.T.V. So, the comedy boom arrived with clubs sprouting in pubs, cellars, warehouses and even in the open air of Covent Garden. Jongleurs in Camden Lock is well worth a visit and The Canal Café in Little Venice features a satirical News Revue. They are always looking for new writers - so if you are a budding Ben Elton you could try your hand.

Eddie Izzard: A very funny guy and a cross - dresser.

Comedy Clubs

Aztec Comedy Club
Borderland Restaurant
47-49 Westow Street SE19
Tel: 0181 771 0885
BR: Crystal Palace/Gypsy Hill
Open: Fri & Sun: Doors 8.30pm, Show
Fri 9.30pm and Sun 9pm;
Mostly stand up old-style and
alternative comedy. Food is available
upstairs as well as in the lively
Mexican restaurant downstairs.

Canal Café Theatre
Bridge House Delamere Terrace W2
Tel: 0171 289 6054
U:Warwick Avenue
Open:Tues-Sun Show 7.30pm
Wed-Sun Different show at 10pm
Late bar food available. Primarily a
fringe theatre but with resident news
revue Thursday-Sunday.

Comedy Store
Haymarket House Oxenden St SW1
Tel: 01426 914433
U: Piccadilly Circus
Shows Tues-Sun 8pm plus second
show at midnight Fri & Sat. Doors
open an hour before show.
Reservations can't be made so be
prepared to arrive early and queue.
Wednesday & Saturday nights are
particularly busy, due to the high
quality improvisation of the famous
Comedy Store Players.

Comedy Café
66 Rivington Street EC2
Tel: 0171 739 5706
U: Old Street (exit 3)

Open: Wed & Thurs Doors 7.30pm,
Show 8.30pm, Bar till 1am, No cover;
Fri & Sat Doors 5pm Show 8.30pm,
Disco/Karaoke -2 30am Incorporates
a range of comedy styles. Wednesday:
Try-Out Night, when the audience
reaction decides which of the new
performers wins a paid booking.

Oranje Boom-Boom Cabaret
Upstairs at De Hems,
Macclesfield Street W1
U: Oxford Circus
Tel: 0171 275 0118
Wed only: Doors 7.45 Show 8.45pm
A high standard of comedy with
4-5 comics featured each evening.

The Improv
161 Tottenham Court Road W1
Telephone 0171 344 4000 Happy hour
7pm-8pm; Show at 8pm Tickets £10
Comedy and cabaret club playing host
to some of the best in transatlantic
comedy and cabaret from Britain and
the USA. Friday and Saturday are
stand up nights with a line-up of
established and alternative comics
plus dancing to resident band and
sounds from Olly the Orange.
Food served throughout the evening.

Jongeleurs Battersea
The Cornet
49 Lavender Gardens SW11
Tel: 0171 924 2766
Weekends only. Fri Doors 8pm; Show
9.15pm; Sat Doors 6pm & 10.30pm
Shows 7.15 & 11.15 pm.
Top comedy club featuring the best of
the comedy circuit. Cover includes free
entrance to the club (open till 2am).
Late bar, and food available. Booking
advisable.

Jongleurs Camden Lock
Dingwalls Building Middle Yard
Camden Lock NW1
Tel: 0171 924 2766
Comedy at weekends only.
Fri doors 7.30pm, show 8.45pm;
Sat Doors 6pm and 10.30pm;
Shows 7.15pm and 11.30pm.
Club open 11pm-2am.
One of the best attended comedy
venues in London, and deservedly so.
The highly appealing bills feature the
best of the comedy circuit. Booking
advisable.

Downstairs at the Kings Head
2 Crouch End Hill
Finsbury Park N8
Tel: 0181 340 1028
Open: Comedy shows on Tues, Wed,
Sat, Sun; show 8pm.
One of the oldest London clubs
offering a variety of comedy styles:
'Outspoken' on Tuesday. This is based
on the interpretation of the written
word. Try-out night featuring new(ish)
acts every second Thursday; weekly
shows on Saturday and Sunday for
the more established performers.

The Hackney Empire
291 Mare Street Hackney E8
Tel: 0181 985 2424
Box office:open between 10am-6pm.
24hour booking line: 0171 420 0000
This venue definitely has star appeal
and many comedy names appear here
as well as those stopping off on tour.
Phone the box office for full details or
check in Time Out the weekly listings
magazine.

The Hampstead Comedy Club
The Washington Englands Lane NW3
Tel: 0171 207 7256
Comedy on Sat only from 8pm.
This club has taken off 'big time' and
is now well established as an
important venue for all promising
stand-ups to play. For reservations
ring the above number on the day of
the show -between 3.30pm-6.30pm.

THEATRELAND CAR PARK
VOUCHER SCHEME

The City of Westminster and
The Society of London Theatre offer
West End theatregoers the opportunity to
park at the specially reduced evening rate of
£3.00 at five MasterPark car parks: Cambridge
Circus, Poland Street, Rochester Row,
Trafalgar and Whitcomb.

For Saturday matinees, theatregoers can park
for £3.00 for a maximum of six hours at the
above car parks plus Cavendish Square Car
Park.

To obtain a car park voucher, request one at
the time you purchase your theatre tickets or
ask the theatre manager when you attend the
performance.

For more information
and a free Westminster Car Parks Map,
call 0800 243348.

Jazz

Note: The club scene is very diverse and constantly changing. The listings below are a small selection of some of the best and/or more established clubs.
For general enquiries and up to date information please telephone the venue.

Blues West 14 Club
11 Russell Gardens W14
Tel: 0171 603 7878
Live music Wed - Sun mainly Blues and some Jazz. 8pm-2am. Licensed Bar & Restaurant & Dancing.
One of London's favourite haunts for top musicians. It is the only American style 'live music' club in London which will transport you across the Atlantic. Well known artists perform; Geno Washington, John Martyn, Ronnie Wood, Hank Marvin - it's a warm and intimate little venue with the artists performing just a few yards away from you.

Bulls Head
373 Lonsdale Road Barnes SW13
Tel: 0181 876 5241
Open daily. Celebrated jazz pub on the river in Barnes, with excellent modern and mainstream music each evening

Bob's Goodtime Blues Bar
41 Brambley Road W10
Opposite Latimer Road tube station.
Tel: 0171 727 4053
Open Mon-Sat 9pm-11pm;
Sun 12noon-3pm; 8.30pm-10.30pm.
Live blues bands every night.

China Jazz
29-31 Parkway
Camden NW1
Tel: 0171 482 4104
Open: 1230-3pm & 6.30-11.30 pm;
Sat 12.30-3pm only.
Recipes gleaned from all over China with no particular regional emphasis. Lavish '20/'30s decor, hand-made noodles and live jazz.

Jazz Café
5 Parkway
Camden Town NW1
Tel: 0171 284 4358
The Original Jazz Café
56 Newington Green Road N16
What used to be a butcher's shop is now a quirky wine bar, cheap and crowded, with an international selection of artists performing three or four nights a week.

100 Club
100 Oxford Street W1
Tel: 0171 636 0933
Open: Mon-Thurs 7.30pm -12.00am;
Fri 8.30pm-3am Sat 7.30pm-1.00am;
Sun 7.30pm-11.30pm
From the Sex Pistols to the Stones, this smoke-filled, steamy basement club has played host to them all. Today the line-up is more jazz and blues with a restaurant serving excellent Caribbean food.

Pizza Express & Pizza on the Park
10 Dean Street, W1
Tel: 0171 437 9595/8722
Open: Tues-Sun 8pm - 1am.
Not just pizza parlours but first class jazz basements enjoying visits from many top names.

Ronnie Scotts
47 Frith Street Soho W1
Tel: 0171 439 0747
Open: Mon-Sat 8.30pm-3.00am
This is the premier jazz venue of the
capital and despite the sad loss of its
founder/owner some time ago,
the club continues to attract the big
names on the jazz circuit.

Soho Pizzeria
16-18 Beak Street W1
Tel: 0171 434 2480
Open 12noon - 12midnight
A relaxing restaurant where the
resident musicians let swing each
evening between 8pm to 12pm, except
Tuesday nights when visitors play the
sets.

606 Club
90 Lots Road Chelsea SW10
Tel: 0171 352 5953
Open nightly 8pm-2am
Late night basement club where
young up-and-coming musicians are
encouraged to play alongside more
established names. Note: they can
only serve alcohol with meals.

Bass Clef
5 Coronet St (off Hoxton Square) N1
Tel: 0171 729 2476/729 2440
Open: Tues-Sun 8.00pm-2.00am
This bohemian backstreet club is
London's training ground for the up-
and-coming, the no-frills alternative to
Ronnie Scott's. The stage area looks
like an empty, subterranean garage
but there's a cosy restaurant serving
good, value- for- money food.

The Troubadour
265 Old Brompton Road SW5
Tel: 0171 370 1434
Open 8.30am-3pm 5.30pm-11pm
Bohemian bar committed to the promotion of esoteric ideas, frequented by
artists, designers, actors, writers and
musicians. Live music, including
flamenco guitar, as well as plays,
poetry readings and discussion. Weird
instruments adorn the walls and
dozens of coffee pots partly obscure
the windows.

Palookaville
13a James Street Covent Garden WC2
Tel: 0171 437 9595
Open: Daily from 12noon to midnight
Variety of good wines and beers available, along with restaurant and entertainment facilities (live mellow jazz).

Dover Street Restaurant Bar
8-10 Dover Street (off Piccadilly) W1
Tel: 0171 629 9813
Situated in the heart of Mayfair
a deceptively modest doorway conceals
the capacious yet intimate delights of
Dover Street. Until the early hours
diners can enjoy a heady blend of live
music whilst choosing from a tempting
French/ Mediterranean menu and
extensive wine list. A winning
combination which cannot fail to please.

Eating Out

Dinner Dances originated in the period after the First World War, during the 'Roaring Twenties'. They evolved from the so-called the dansant, or tea dances, which although popular with the ladies were less so with gentlemen, who were obliged to combine waltzing with working during the afternoon.

At first Dinner Dances were an aristocratic phenomenon, held in the great private houses of the day, both in London and in the country where they might be combined with weekend house parties. Formal invitations on thick white card, edged in gold and with print in high relief would invite guests to dine and dance usually from 8pm until around midnight, although particularly grand dances, such as coming out balls or those to celebrate a debutantes' presentation at Court might continue until dawn, and sometimes breakfast would even be served the following morning to the most determined revellers.

Dinner dances at this time were high fashion occasions where the glitterati amongst the great and the well born would glitter and shine. Ladies might wear the latest in long, ankle length "flapper" dresses, with a velvet band around the head and perhaps a feather boa or a flower in the hair. Long strings of beads, knotted above the waist, and elongated cigarette holders were the height of chic, and the smoke of Turkish cigarettes would mingle with the sweet scents of Diorissima.

It was an era when jewellery was worn in abundance, pearl chokers at the neck, drop-like pendant earrings, and exquisite necklaces, rings and bracelets. The gentlemen would be soberly dinner-jacketed, unless dressing for a grand London ball when tails and white tie would be worn.

Royalty would often attend grand dances at which times the ladies' elbow length gloves would always be white.

La Concordia Notte: One of the few remaining dinner dance restaurants in central London

The favourite couturier of the Royal Family and for ladies of the highest familes was Norman Hartnell. His dress creations set the tone and style for a generation and a now long vanished epoch.

As the slow diminuendo of the aristocracy gathered pace throughout the twentieth century, Dinner Dances too felt the wind of change. To meet less abundant fortunes, Dinner Dances began to be held in the great hotels of the capital. Hostesses would issue invitations for dances at one of London's Great Hotels, all of which offered dining facilities, dance floors and their own in-house bands or orchestras.

Everyone had a favourite venue, be it the Ritz, the Savoy or the old Berkeley Hotel; Hatchets was popular, as was The 400, which was a members only nightclub; the Hungaria was on Lower Regent Street, and the Mayfair just off Berkeley Square. Another favourite was the Cafe de Paris in Leicester Square which was tragically bombed during the War taking with it half of London's high society.

The London hotels offered sumptuous surroundings for Dinner Dances. Some were all red plush carpets, velvet curtains, flock wallpaper, gilt mirrors on the walls, sparkling chandeliers and groves of potted palms; others were light, bright and brilliantly lit with tables grouped around a small, closely packed dance floor. A new generation of couturier arose, Hardy Amies, Balmain, Balenciaga and Dior. Cocktail dresses of taffeta were all the rage and the men relaxed a little into three piece suits. World War 2 marked the watershed of the Dinner Dance; attempts were made during the 1950's to revive the pre-war

gaiety but times had changed and in a more austere world the heady style of the Dinner Dance no longer suited people's life-styles or their purses. Nonetheless in the immediate post-war era women who had spent the five years of the war in the Women's Land Army, wearing trousers and breeches, leapt at the opportunity offered by the bang up to date calf length hemlines of Norman Hartnell's "New Look" of 1947. Just as people had their favourite venues, so they also had their dance band of choice. Amongst the most popular were the orchestras of Joe Loss, Mantovani and Tommy Dorsey.

But over the decades an inexorable decline set in. The Beatles at the Cavern Club and Rock & Roll ensured that the younger generation of the 50's would dance to a different beat.

The age of the private Dinner Dance was waning, to be replaced by smaller more intimate restaurants where couples and small groups of friends might go to dine and dance. The Sixties - hip, cool and rebellious - subverted a new generation away from Dinner Dances and an element of nostalgia began to creep in.

Today there are a small number of restaurants which specifically offer these evenings, such as the Concordia Notte. The music may be electronic, or even pre-recorded. and dress is as informal as you like. Nonetheless the days of Palm Court dancing are not quite over: one can still catch an echo of the charleston and the quick step, of foxtrots and waltzes, of the Roaring Twenties and the Jazz Age, in some of the grander London hotels.

Classic

The Belvedere
Holland House Holland Park W8
(entrance in Abbotsbury Road)
Tel: 0171 602 1238
Mon-Sat Noon-3pm & 7pm-11pm;
Sun lunch only. 12 noon-3pm
Possibly the most romantic setting for
a restaurant in London: a beautiful
17th century orangery with views of
Holland Park. The cuisine is best
described as 'Modern British' and is
informal yet elegant.

Bistrot 190
190 Queen's Gate SW7
Tel: 0171 581 5666
Open: Mon-Sat 11am-11pm;
Sun: Lunch 12noon-3pm
This popular eatery buzzes with
lively, arty types. The dining room is
very British with elegant high
ceilings, prints and dried flowers on
the walls in a delightful atmosphere.
Amiable service, fair pricing and well
executed Mediterranean fare to boot.

Connaught Restaurant
Carlos Place, W1
Tel: 0171 499 7070
Open: Daily 12.30pm-2.30pm and
6.30pm-10.30pm
Housed in the famous hotel; spacious
with beautiful wood panelling, but
not the expense account venue one
might expect. Fine traditional
English and French food (notably
game) The puddings, such as port
jelly, are a real delight.

Leith's
92 Kensington Park Road W11
Tel: 0171 229 4481
Open: Mon-Sat 7pm-11.30pm
Sun: 6.30pm-10pm
Situated in a handsome Victorian
terraced house, Prue Leith's superb
restaurant enjoys the patronage of
dedicated businessmen and locals.
Leith's duckling comes highly
recommended, as does her fine
vegetarian menu.

Chutney Mary: A truly magnificent dining experience

Celebrity Spots

Daphne's
112 Draycott Avenue SW3
Tel: 0171 589 4257
Daily Noon-3pm and 7pm-11.30pm
Popular again under ownership who
are achieving their aim of restoring
the chîc and fashionable reputation.
Garden room with retractable glass
roof and Italian/ Mediterranean
menu.

The Ivy
1 West Street Covent Garden WC2
Tel: 0171 836 4751
Daily Noon-3pm and 5.30pm-
Midnight (last orders)
Popular Covent Garden restaurant,
ideally located for theatre-goers. Wood
panelling and stained glass add to the
atmosphere, while top class
international cuisine is on offer for
the elegant and fashionable clientele.

Joe Allen
13 Exeter Street Covent Garden WC2
Tel: 0171 836 0651
Mon-Sat Noon-1am Sun Midnight
One of London's major thespian
eating houses, attracting actors from
the West End shows; serves American
fare with flair. The waiters tend to be
quite offhand - if not downright rude,
but some people say this is all an act.
But just in case, be on your guard for
the malignant thrust and be prepared
for engaging répartee

Langan's Brasserie
Stratton Street Near Green Park W1
Tel: 0171 493 6437
Open: Mon-Fri 12.30-2.30pm and
7-11.30pm and Sat 8pm-midnight.
Co-founded by Michael Caine, this
large, well-known restaurant is still
one of the showbiz meeting places.
Has a great atmosphere and a menu
with over 60 selections which change
daily. The waiters can be a bit surly
and over-eager with the wine pouring,
but otherwise it's fun.

San Lorenzo
22 Beauchamp Place SW3
Tel: 0171 584 9850
Open Mon-Sat 12.30pm-3pm and
7.30pm-11.30pm
Well-established home from home for
the well-heeled, celebs, Chelsea
footballers and their wives and ladies
who lunch. Most of the regulars have
a favourite table and Eric Clapton's
happens to be 21. The usual band of
dedicated 'snappers' are to be spotted
lurking outside.

Circus
1 Upper James Street
Tel: 0171 534 4000
Open Mon-Fri for lunch between 12-3
and dinner 6pm-11pm
Closed Sunday
Modern European cooking, with the
accent on taste, texture and season-
ality, served in a streamlined setting
that thrives on a classical air.

Santini
29 Ebury Street SW1
Tel: 0171 730 4094
Open Mon-Fri 12.30pm-2.30pm and
7pm-11.30 Sat 7pm-11.30pm and
Sun 7pm-10.30
A wonderfully stylish restaurant
where you may savour authentic
Italian cooking. It seems to attract a
great many people from the world of
showbiz. Barbra Streisand's always
dines here when she visits London.

Quaglino's
16 Bury Street SW1
Tel: 0171 930 6767
Mon-Sun Noon-3.00pm ;
Sun-Thu 5.30pm - midnight;
Fri & Sat 5.30pm-12.30am .
Much talked about place to see and
be seen, although the general
consensus of opinion on the food
itself is that it's not overwhelming.
Completely redesigned in grand style
with sweeping staircase, rich colours,
individually designed columns and
dramatic crustacea altar filled with
pyramids of sea creatures.

Zinc Bar and Grill
21 Heddon Street W1
Tel: 0171 255 8899
Superlative new offering from gastro-
guru Sir Terence Conran, with a 12m
zinc bar for classic cocktails, while
the menu spans grills, salads and
crustacea.

The Pharmacy in Notting Hill Gate

Celebrity Spots

Planet Hollywood
13 Coventry Street Piccadilly W1
Tel: 0171 287 1000
Open Mon-Fri 11.30am-1am .
Sat & Sun 11am-1am
What can one say about this much hyped restaurant except that it's one of the largest restaurants in London with three floors covering 25,000 square feet and 450 seats. Numerous items of movie memorabilia are on display. The cuisine is Californian and turns out to be more than 'passable'.

The Collection
264 Brompton Road SW3
Tel: 0171 225 1212
Open daily for lunch and dinner.
Mogens Tholstrup has added this mega fashionable restaurant to his vastly popular Daphne's. This superb former fashion warehouse is on two floors with a long bar. The food is a mix of European and Asian.

The Avenue
7-9 St James's Street SW1
Tel: 0171 321 2111
Open for lunch and dinner.
This restaurant opened its doors to the public back in 1996 and has become one of the most fashionable places to dine. Every attention is paid to detail and it has a truly magnificent atmosphere. Booking well in advance is essential.

Dover Street Restaurant Bar
8-10 Dover Street off Piccadilly W1
Tel: 0171 629 9813
Established as one of London's most atmospheric restaurants and live music venues for almost twenty years. Recently underwent major refurbishment to create three new bars.It is as serious about the food as the music. It is also one of the capital's best value lunchtime venues with imaginative French/ Mediterranean cuisines in the evening, together with a lively mixture of top jazz, R &B and soul bands and resident DJ's.

Dover Street Restaurant and Bar: Where good food and music meet on equal terms

English

Fredericks
Camden Passage Islington N1
Tel: 0171 359 2888
Open daily 6pm-11.30pm
(Last Orders)
This fine eatery has been consistently good over the past decade and is extremely popular with the Islington set, business people and serious foodies. An excellent wine list complements the fine French cooking served in an elegant dining room. An area is reserved for smokers and booths for the romantically inclined. An ideal venue for that really very special occasion.

Maggie Jones
Old Court Place
Kensington Church Street W8
Tel: 0171 937 6462
Mon-Sat 12.30-am 2.30 pm &7pm-1130pm Sun 6.30pm-1100pm
Authentic English farmhouse restaurant with pine dressers and wooden tables and the best apple crumbles and treacle tarts in town!

Orrery
55-57 Marylebone High Street W1
Tel: 0171 616 8000.
Mon- Sun for lunch 12noon-3pm
Dinner 7pm-11pm
Sir Terence Conran has triumphed yet again, with this intimate, neighbourhood restaurant serving classic and contemporary dishes overlooking the beautiful Marylebone Church gardens.

Pharmacy Restaurant
150 Notting Hill Gate W11
Tel: 0171 221 2442
Mon-Sun 12noon -3pm and 6.45pm -10.45
The restaurant design concept is by Damien Hirst. Medicine cabinets line the walls of the ground floor and contain drug packaging. The top of the bar stools are in the shape of white tablets and the food is best described as English with Pan-European and Pacific influences. Quite an experience.

Rules Restaurant
35 Maiden Lane WC2
Telephone: 0171 836 5314
Mon-Sat 12.noon-11.30pm;
Sun 12 noon 10.30pm
This is one of the oldest restaurants in London and one of the most celebrated in the world. Unique historical interior with private rooms available for hire. Traditional English cooking at its very best, specialising in classic game cookery, oysters, pies and puddings.

Veronica's Restaurant
3 Hereford Road
Off Westbourne Grove W2
Tel: 0171 229 5079
Lunch Mon - Fri 12 noon -2.30-pm
Dinner Mon -Sat 6pm -11.30pm
A charming, intimate and friendly restaurant offering their own imaginative interpretations of classic 'home made' English cooking.

European

Fish

The Square
6-10 Bruton Street W1
Tel: 0171 495 7100
Mon-Fri 12Noon-2.45pm; Mon-Sat
6pm -11.45pm; Sun 7pm-10.30pm
This fashionable restaurant serves
modern British/European cuisine to a
young, chic clientele. Many claim that
this is the best place to eat and 'be
seen'.

First Floor
186 Portobello Road W11
Tel: 0171 243 0072
Open Mon-Sat 10am-4pm and 7pm -
11.30pm Sun 12noon-9pm
This upmarket eatery serves
Continental cuisine to a crowd of
"young, trendy groovers". Models and
pop stars can be spotted dining in
"pseudo-classical" surroundings. The
loud music seems to please some and
worry others.

Livebait
21 Wellington Street WC2
Tel: 0171 836 7161
Open: Mon-Sat 12noon -.3pm and
5.30pm 11.30pm
Wonderful fish and seafood dishes in
this now a very fashionable place to
dine, either before or after the show.

Sea Shell
49-51 Lisson Grove NW1
Tel: 0171 723 8703
Mon-Sat 12noon-10.30pm
Sun 12noon-3pm
One of London's most popular fish
and chip restaurants. The produce
is purchased fresh from Billingsgate
Market each dawn. The chips are
fried in healthy groundnut oil but
sadly you can no longer bring your
own wine. Well worth a visit .

The very popular Deals Restaurant

French

Le Gavroche
43 Upper Brook Street W1
Tel: 0171 408 0881
Mon-Fri Noon-2pm & 7pm-11pm
This mecca of gastronomy enjoys
patronage from businessmen around
the world. One of the finest
restaurants in the country, now in the
hands of Michel Roux Jnr.

La Pomme d'Amour
128 Holland Park Avenue W11
Tel: 0171 229 8532
Mon-Fri 12.30-2.15pm and Mon-Sat
7pm-10.45pm
You will find this very French
eatery in this tree-lined avenue in
Holland Park - which always reminds
one of Paris. A fabulous, leafy
conservatory, an elegantly decorated
dining room - both creating a
wonderful ambience. A selection of
contemporary dishes as well as
excellent wine is to be enjoyed.

Greek

Kalamaras
76-78 Inverness Mews Off Queensway W2
Tel: 0171 727 9122
Open: Mon-Sat 7pm - midnight
Hidden away in this tiny mews off
Queensway you will find this fine
Greek restaurant. They serve
traditional food (of the mainland)
with excellent salads and delicacies.
They also have a pretty extensive
Greek wine list and a separate room
for private parties. Packed most
evenings so it would be advisable to
book before going along.

Indian

Chutney Mary
535 Kings Road SW10
Tel: 0171 351 3113
Open: Seven days between 7pm-11pm
Awarded 'Top Indian' restaurant in
Britain and a red 'M' by Michelin, for
five years running. It is beautiful and
stylish with large Anglo-Indian
murals and garden conservatory.
Applauded for its gourmet dishes
from the various regions of India. Try
Calamari chilli fry or spicy roast
shark of lamb.

Royals
7-8 Bow Street Covent Garden WC2
Tel: 0171 379 1099
Mon-Sat 12noon-2.30pm; 5.30 -
12mid- night. Sun 5pm-11pm
This restaurant is well placed for
theatregoers and with an attractive
'set menu' comprising of North Indian
and Kashmir dishes both mild and
strong and is extremely good value.

Spices
18 Chilworth Street
Near Paddington Station W2
Tel: 0171 706 8588
Open Mon-Sat 12noon-2.30pm; 6pm-
11.30pm and Sun 12.30pm-3pm and
6pm -11pm
The menu is conventional serving
Balti and Tandoori dishes. The decor
is easy on the eye and the main
visual diversion is provided by
turquoise tablecloths over pink
undercloths. The waiting staff are
efficient and polite. The restaurant is
off the beaten track and it seems to
attract most of its business from the
local area.

Indian

Star of India
154 Old Brompton Road SW5
Tel: 0171 373 2901
Website: www.starofindia.co.uk
12noon-3pm Mon-Sat 6pm-Midnight
Sun 7pm-11.30pm
This restaurant has been established
for 47 years and was rewarded by
both the Evening Standard and
Carlton Television in their restaurant
awards. First-class cuisine that's in a
class of its own, Baingan-E-Bahar-
Baked aubergine steaks stuffed with
cottage cheese, and sesame seeds
topped with diced tomatoes, in
particular is highly recommended.
It takes twenty minutes preparation
time but it is well worth the wait.

Vijay
49 Willesden Lane NW6
Tel: 0171 328 1087/328 1982
Sun -Thu 6.10.45 Fri-Sat 6 pm 11.45
Open: 6pm-10.45pm 7 days
It is always a good sign to find the
same staff in the same restaurant for
a number of years this quality
Southern Indian eatery can make this
proud boast. Most evenings you will
find turban and sari-clad customers
who have travelled some considerable
distance to eat here.

International

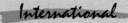

Pomegranates
94 Grosvenor Road SW1
Tel: 0171 828 6560
Open: Mon-Fri Noon-2.15pm
Mon-Sat 7pm-11.15pm

Definitely one of London's best-kept
secrets, with a clientele of celebs,
politicians and businessmen. With
dishes from around the world the
international team of chefs make for
an extensive and very eclectic menu
and is one of the most romantic
settings in town.

Deals
"Food from around the world that
doesn't cost the earth." Established in
1988. Deals is a popular restaurant
and bar offering an exciting mix of
contemporary, American and Pan
Asian cuisine with one of the most
famous cocktail lists in London.
Friday and Saturday late night music
and dancing at Deals Soho with Deals
Chelsea Harbour and Hammersmith
offering ideal weekend and family
venues.

Deals at Chelsea Harbour
Harbour Yard SW10
Tel: 0171 795 1001
Mon-Sat 12noon -3.30pm; and 5pm
10.30pm; Sun 12noon -4pm

Deals at Soho
14-16 Fouberts Place W1
Tel: 0171 287 1001
Mon- Thu 12noon -11.30pm; Fri -Sat
12noon-1.30am; Sun 12noon-5pm

Deals at Hammersmith
Bradmore House
Queen Caroline Street W6
Tel: 0181 563 1001
Mon- Thu 12noon -3pm; and 5pm -11pm
Fri-Sat 12noon-11pm; Sun 12-3pm

Irish

Lindsay House
21 Romilly Street
Soho W1
Tel: 0171 439 0450
Mon-Fri Lunch 12noon-2.30pm
Mon-Sat Dinner 6pm-11pm
This 18th century former private
residence in the heart of Soho is now
a stylish home to the modern Irish
cooking of chef Richard Corrigan.

Minogue's
80 Liverpool Road
Islington N1
Tel: 0171 354 4440
Open Tue-Sat 11am -3pm and 6pm-
11pm Sun 12noon-3pm (for lunch
only) Very basic traditional Irish fare
with a lot of seafood dishes, beef and
lamb, most of which are cooked in
Guinness or Irish whisky.

Italian

L'Incontro
87 Pimlico Road SW1
Tel: 0171 730 3663
Open: Mon-Fri 12.30pm-2.30pm and
7pm-11.30pm; Sat 7pm-11.30pm;
Closed Sun
One of the most expensive but elegant
restaurants in town. Often described
as Venice-on-the-Thames. Regulars
include David Bowie, Nick Faldo and
Al Pacino.

Barbarella Restaurant
428 Fulham Road SW6
Tel: 0171 385 9434
Open Mon-Sat 7.30pm-3am
Dine and dance to disco music in this
60's style nightspot. The restaurant is
situated quite close to the Chelsea
Football ground and you occasionally
spot some of the team enjoying a
drink, or drowning their sorrows at
the bar after a poor result.

The moody but quite brilliant Jean Christophe Novelli the proud owner of Michelin starred
Novellis at 30 Clerkenwell Green EC1

Italian

Bertorelli's Cafe Italian
19 Charlotte Street W1
Near British Telecom Tower
Tel: 0171 637 4174
Open: Mon-Sat for lunch and dinner .
Last orders 11pm
Home of the original Bertorelli
brothers restaurant that was first
established in 1913. The restaurant
underwent major refurbishment and
now has a very sleek look indeed. The
food on offer here is modern Italian
and the prices are reasonable, by West
End standards. The service is brisk
both upstairs and downstairs. The
restaurant is also available for private
party hire.

Concordia Restaurant
29-31 Craven Road W2
Tel: 0171 723 3725
Mon-Sat 12 -3pm and 6pm-11.45pm
This is the upstairs restaurant of the
Militello Brothers famous Concordia
Notte. It has an extensive traditional
menu and a comprehensive wine list.
It attracts a good lunch time trade
from the local advertising agencies
and the Football Association's
hierarchy from nearby Lancaster Gate.

L'Accento
16 Garway Road
Off Westbourne Grove W2
Tel: 0171 243 2201/2664
Open Mon-Fri 12.30pm-2.15pm
Mon-Sun 6.30pm-11.00pm
This compact but very airy
restaurant, continues to serve
'Modern Italian' food that is both good
and as modestly priced. Booking well
in advance is recommended

Verbanella
30 Beauchamp Place SW3
Tel: 0171 584 1107
Open seven days a week from:-
12noon-3pm and 6pm- 11.30pm
This popular restaurant within a
shopping throw of Harrods is run by
the charming Giulio Comoli, who has
been a restaurateur for almost forty
years. The eatery is set on two levels;
in this busy 'shop -till you drop' street
- that has possibly the highest
concentration of restaurants in the
entire of London. Decorated in airy
soft pastels and serving excellent
traditional cuisine, including home-
made pastas.

Japanese

Shiki
27 Davies Street W1
Tel: 0171 409 0750
Open: Mon-Sat 12.30pm-2.30pm
and 6.30pm-10.30pm
Kimono-clad waitresses serving an
authentic Japanese menu in an
atmosphere of sheer elegance. Sushi
bar upstairs, full menu in the
restaurant downstairs, plus three
private rooms.

Benihana
77 Kings Road Chelsea SW3
Tel: 0171 376 7799
Open: Mon-Sun 12noon-3pm and
6pm-11pm
A unique dining experience may be
had in this Western-style Japanese
restaurant.

The cuisine is Teppenyaki style,
where the food is cooked in front of
you as you sit around the griddle
watching the extrovert chefs perform.

Lebanese

Fakhreldine Restaurant
85 Piccadilly W1
Tel: 0171 493 3424
Open: Daily 12noon-1am
A very elegant dining room and
exceptional views overlooking Green
Park await you when you visit one of
London's finest Lebanese
restaurants. A large variety of hors
d'oeuvres and kebabs prepared in the
traditional way, with an extensive
wine list which includes Lebanese.

The dining room downstairs of Terence Conran's **Mezzo** Restaurant in Wardour Street

Mexican

Down Mexico Way
25 Swallow Street (off Regent Street)
Near Piccadilly W1
Tel: 0171 437 9895
Rest: Mon-Sat noon-midnight
Bar is open until 3am
Beautifully designed Mexican
restaurant with fountain, plants, cacti
and Spanish tiles, hand painted fifty
or more years ago in Seville. The
entertainment is provided by Latin
American dancers. A wild night to be
had by all.

Peking

Emperor
368-370 King's Road Chelsea SW3
Tel: 0171 352 6797
Daily:Noon-Midnight
Peking and Cantonese dishes served
to a lively, mainly young, clientele at
reasonable prices. Very popular, with
dishes modified to suit Western
palates. Monkfish (Five Willows Fish)
and grilled chicken Peking style are
among regional dishes on offer.

Mr Wing
242 Old Brompton Road SW5
Tel: 0171 370 2624
Open:1pm-Midnight daily
Exquisite Peking/Cantonese cuisine
in extraordinary tropical plant-filled
surroundings with exotic fish
residing in a tank to one side and an
ornamental fish pond to the other.
Intimate alcoves and there's also a
room for banquets.

Romantic

The Canteen
Chelsea Harbour SW10
Tel: 0171 351 7330
Open: Mon-Sat 12noon-3pm; 7-12pm;
Sun 12.30-3.30 pm and 7pm-11.30
Another of Michael Caine's
gastronomic ventures whose followers
have already made this the place to
be seen. International menu with
excellent views of the harbour.

Concordia Notte
29-31 Craven Road W2
Tel: 0171 402 4985
Open: Mon-Sat 9pm-2.30am
Traditional - style Italian restaurant
with an extensive menu and wine list.
Enjoyed most of its popularity in the
boom years of the mid 80's. but
nevertheless has a loyal following.
From 8.30pm nightly you can enjoy
dinner and dancing to a live band -
and this seems to be very popular
with people from the world of show
biz, soap opera queens and Arab
princes who arrive nightly with their
entire entourage.

The Conservatory
The Lanesborough Hotel
Hyde Park Corner SW1
Tel: 0171 259 5599
Open: Fri-Sat 8.30pm-12-15am
Dancing: Music is provided by the
resident live trio
Three course set dinner £33
House wine at around £17
The glass-ceilinged conservatory
room (styled on the Brighton Pavilion)
with its fine Oriental decor all adds
up to being an extremely popular
dinner/dance venue.

Romantic

Memories of China
Chelsea Harbour SW10
Tel: 0171 352 4953
Open: Mon-Sat 12noon -2.30pm; 7pm
-10.45pm; Sun 12.30-10pm
One of the first restaurants to appear
in the prestigious Chelsea Harbour
development when it opened in 1988.
The cuisine is first class, prepared by
specialist chefs from Hong Kong.

The River Café
Rainville Road
Hammersmith W6
Tel: 0171 381 8824
Open: Mon-Sat Lunch 12.30pm-
2.30pm; Dinner 7.30pm-11pm;
Sun (lunch only) 1pm-2.30pm
Northern Italian menu in chic café
surroundings. It has been described
as a "true destination restaurant
whose unfussy cooking epitomises the
mood of the times" and we couldn't
agree more.

The Terrace
Le Meridien Hotel
Piccadilly Circus W1
Tel: 0171 465 1642
Open for breakfast Mon Sat 7am-
10.30am Sun 7.30am-11am
Lunch:12noon-2.30pm;
Afternoon teas 3pm-5.30;
Dinner 6pm-11pm; Sun 6pm -10.30pm.
On the second floor you will find the
atmosphere sophisticated, restrained
and very elegant: understatedly
Parisian, and to English eyes 'very
Terence Conran'. The new chef Michel
Rostang is a symbol of contemporary
French culinary culture.
We particularly liked a central table
with three tall swan necked vases
containing identical sprays of white
lilies. Everything feels spacious and
uncluttered. The service is attentive
but discreet and unobtrusive. An ideal
eatery for before or after theatre
dining.

The elegant **Terrace Restaurant** in the Meridien Hotel Piccadilly Circus.

Romantic

Blue Print Café
Butlers Wharf, SE1.
Tel: 0171 378 7031
Open: Mon-Sat 12-3 6.30-10.45pm
Sun 12-3.15pm
Actually part of the Design Museum above which it is located. This eatery has really fabulous views of the Thames and Tower Bridge and a fine cosmopolitan menu. A good spot for a romantic dinner or a lazy Sunday lunch.

Gavin's
5 Lacy Road Putney SW15
Tel: 0181 785 9151
12Noon-3.30pm and 6pm-11pm
Situated just off the High Street, this thriving neighbourhood restaurant specialises in fresh pasta made daily on the premises, plus interesting brasserie cooking. Good vibes and good value

The Gaudi Restaurant: your table awaits youi

Spanish

The Depot
Tideway Yard
Mortlake High Street SW14
Tel: 0181 878 9462
Daily 12noon-3pm and 6pm-11pm
It may take some finding but the trek is well-rewarded by a stunning position on the river and an electric atmosphere. Good cooking and a comprehensive wine list at reasonable prices. River views and a good buzz.

Gaudi Restaurant
63b Clerkenwell Road EC1
Tel:0171 608 3220.
Open Mon Fri 12noon 2.30pm and 7pm-10.30pm; Sat 7pm.-1030pm
The use of mobile phones is prohibited. Gaudi is a stunning addition to the London Restaurant scene. John Newtttan has created a decor which is as unique as the cuisine of chef Nacho Martinez-Jiminez is exceptional. There is an open kitchen on the ground floor, presided over by chef Nacho himself; all is calm,unruffled, highly organised and astonishingly quiet: no clatter of pots and pans, no shouted orders, just a sense of serene order and efficiency. Nacho's menu is a dream. The service flowed smoothly and seamlessly as dishes and glasses came and went; the waiters and waitresses were all smart and unobtrusive but friendly and well informed when asked for advice or recommendations. A meal here is a great treat and comes highly recommended. If advice is appropriate: don't decide whether to dine at Gaudi, simply decide when, and the sooner the better.

Thai

Blue Elephant
4-6 Fulham Broadway SW6
Tel: 0171 385 6595
Open Sun-Fri 12noon-2pm and Mon -
Sun 7pm -midnight
This is one of the most romantic
restaurants in which to dine in
London. A king's ransom has been
spent on the exotic flowers and a pool
complete with whispering fountains
adds to the attraction. A wonderful
venue for that special occasion .

Thai Pavilion
42 Rupert Street Piccadilly W1
Tel: 0171 287 6333
Open Mon-Sun 12noon-2.30pm and
6pm-11.30pm (Sunday 10.30pm)
Stylish, authentic cuisine with chair or
Thai-style floor cushion seating.
The restaurant has a set menu for
theatregoers that is extremely good.

Tibetan

The Tibetan Restaurant
17 Irving Street
Leicester Square WC2
Tel: 0171 839 2090
Lunch: Mon-Sat Noon-3pm;
Dinner 5pm-10.45pm. Closed Sun.
Boasts at being the first and only
Tibetan restaurant in the U.K. A small
friendly restaurant with authentic
atmosphere . The menu hosted a
variety of traditional dishes along with
other selections of noodles and soups.
Average price for two (without wine)
is around £25. Well positioned for
before or after theatre dining.

The Hard Rock - Where the music is loud,
and if you are old enough to recognise it, you're old
enough to want it turned down.

Theme Places

Hard Rock Café
160 Old Park Lane Piccadilly W1
Tel: 0171 629 0382
Daily 12 noon to around 1am
A top tourist attraction for over a
quarter of a century. Traditional US
favourites like burgers, ribs and fried
chicken are on the menu. The music
is loud (and rock 'n' roll) and if you
are old enough to recognise it, you're
old enough to want it turned down.
Bric-a-brac adorns the walls.

Theme Places

The Sports Café
80 Haymarket SW1
Tel: 0171 839 8300
Open seven days a week from
Mon-Wed 12noon-2am; Thu-Sat
12noon-3am; Sun 12noon-11pm
Set in 12000 square feet of sporting
activity, this venue comes into its own
during major events. Over one
hundred television sets are screening
sporting action from some part of the
globe, at any given time. Good
atmosphere . during top sporting
events.

Terry Neill's Sports Bar
53 Holborn Viaduct Holborn EC1
Tel: 0171 329 6653
The ex - Arsenal and Spurs player/
manager seems to have found a
winning formula here and looks as
comfortable behind the bar as he was
on the ball. He is also a very congenial
host regardless of whom you support.
A great atmosphere during Internationals.

Sticky Fingers
1a Phillimore Gardens W8
Tel: 0171 938 5338
Open Mon-Sat 12noon-11.30pm;
Sun 12noon-11pm
The diner is owned by ex-Rolling
Stone Bill Wyman. Good quality,
burgers, steaks, tuna melts, pecan pie
and all the usuals on offer and almost
inevitably it seems, the walls are
plastered with 'pop memorabilia'.
The real attraction here seems to be a
nostalgic one - especially if your a
'Stones' fan because you might bump
into Bill entertaining some of his 'old
celebrity chums' from the music biz.

Vegetarian

Food For Thought
31 Neal Street Covent Garden WC2
Tel: 0171 836 0239
An extremely popular vegetarian
eatery which is frequented by local
office types and visitors alike. The
menu changes daily but always
includes stews, quiche salads and stir
fry. They also offer a prompt take-
away service.

Mildreds
58 Greek Street W1
Tel: 0171 494 1634
Open Mon-Sat 11am-11pm
Offers fine vegetarian, and some fish
dishes. Organic produce is used
whenever possible without
preservatives or additives.

Raw Deal
65 York Street Near Baker Street W1
Tel: 0171 262 4841
Open Mon-Sat
Enjoys a very busy lunch-time trade
but is very quiet in the evenings. The
food is moderately priced, service is
slightly impersonal but nevertheless
efficient.

Thali
3-7 Endell Street Covent Garden WC2
Tel: 0171 379 6493
Mon-Sun from 12noon-12midnight.
Situated in the heart of Covent
Garden this fine vegetarian
restaurant offers an all-day buffet for
under £5 or a choice of set menus for
around £8. Well worth a visit.

Pubs

In Muswell Hill in North London recently I came across an old stone-clad Gothic style church with tapering spire. Feeling in need of spiritual sustenance I entered and to my amazement was greeted by pop music and people getting their spiritual uplift from pints of foaming beer.

This former house of God is now a Firkin pub complete with pews, pulpits and massive organ. On the other side of London in Fleet Street, that other deity Mammon the god of money has been converted by Bacchus. He has turned his palatial Old Bank of England into a Fuller's Ale House, the assets now being definitely liquid. All over London former shops, warehouses, banks, railway stations and even cinemas are being converted into pubs,taverns or alehouses, many with a strong foodie element. Theme bars seem to be all the rage at the moment with Irishness at the forefront.

Finnegan's Wake's and O'Neills have sprouted up everywhere offering fake Oirishness. They are run by the big breweries who know a good marketing idea when they see one. Next year will we see Rob Roys and Tam O'Shanters? If you are tired of the trendy, flashy fashion driven scene why not steep yourself in London' s history? Transport yourself back a few centuries and nip into an old coaching inn of the sort you see on Christmas cards. The George near London Bridge is one such and Dickens was also a regular. Dick Turpin, Jack the Ripper, Queen Elizabeth,

Churchill and Charles de Gaulle are other folk from the past you might bump into on your travels or especially after a wee dram.

If you are wandering along Wapping Highway by the Thames you might encounter a pub sign swinging in the breeze depicting a stern looking Captain Kidd. Ironical, for the pirate himself swung from a gibbet a few yards from here, his body to be washed by three tides of the Thames. That other icon of the serial killer, Jack the Ripper, has his favourite haunt in Whitechapel, The Ten Bells. Two of his victims were regulars here but if you visit at certain times you are likely to be greeted by a naked lady who will disrobe artistically. More like Jack the Stripper. As well as ladies practising the 'full monty' you might find pubs where likely lads and lasses hone their comic talents on comedy nights or places where groups perform.

A note on the law

Britain's outdated and inconvenient drinking laws came into being during World War One to tackle excessive drinking by munition factory workers. In 1988 (and not before time) these laws were relaxed. Pubs may now stay open from 11am to 11pm Mon-Sat; Sun 12 noon -10.30pm. Within these restrictions the precise opening times are very much at the individual landlord's discretion. Before the end of each session and ten minutes before closing time the barman either rings a bell or shouts 'let me 'ave your glasses' - The more polite landlord may simply say 'time gentlemen please' and then, you are allowed twenty minutes to finish your drink.

WHATEVER

YOU DO,

TAKE PRIDE.

The Blind Beggar

337 Whitechapel Road E1

This East End boozer was notorious as the scene of the gangland murder of villain George Cornell in the sixties. His assassin marched in and shot him at point blank range. Not only was the beggar blind, but the whole pub must have been, because nobody saw a thing. The East End at that time was in the grip of the Kray Brothers, masters of menace and extortion. Eventually witnesses were persuaded to come forward to testify and so the criminal stranglehold which the Krays had on this part of London came to an end.

Bull and Bush

Richmond (opposite the BR station). In London of the swinging sixties this was where it all happened-musically speaking. The Station Hotel as it then was, boasted the Crawdaddy Club, the South's answer to Liverpool's Cavern. Whereas the Cavern was the birthplace of the Beatles, the Station spawned The Rolling Stones. In 1963 the Stones were the resident band and were paid 22 pounds for their first gig - even the Beatles came here to hear them play. Fame beckoned and the starbound Stones were replaced by the Yardbirds, featuring Eric Clapton, Long John Baldry and the Hoochie Coochie Band, Elton John, Rod Stewart are just a few of the rock legends who got a break here in this roomy, atmospheric pub. On Wednesday nights they have a band. Their name? The Strolling Bones, Mick Jagger still has a pad in the area. Residents more like it.

Burlington Bertie

39-45 Shaftesbury Avenue W1
Tel: 0171 437 0947

This pub in the heart of theatreland is only six years old but looks a period piece with its armchairs and sofas and gallery bar. They used to have a pianist at a grand piano - a "play it again Sam" kind of guy. He's been given the heave-ho and replaced with a more 'techno' organist. Bring back the romance.

Captain Kidd

108 Wapping High Street E1
Tel: 0171 480 5759

As you wander down Wapping Way you will come alongside the Captain Kidd, a fair galleon among sailors taverns. Instead of the Jolly Roger she is flying a portrait of the stern-faced Scottish pirate, William Kidd. He glares down daring you to enter this recently converted Georgian building. Wooden beams abound, recreating the atmosphere of a nautical tavern, or even a ship. The only thing missing is a parrot.

The Coach and Horses

29 Greek Street Soho W1
Tel: 0171 437 5920

Another Soho mecca for bohemians. Famed as the favourite bar of the late Jeffrey Bernard. The landlord Norman Balon does not like tourists, so it is best to go disguised as a native - perhaps wearing a black beret and T-shirt with 'Tourists-Up-Yours!' emblazoned on it.

Compton Arms

4 Compton Ave off Canonbury Lane
Tel: 0171 359 2645

Like a country inn in the heart of
leafy Canonbury. This area of
Islington is popular with actors and
prospective Labour party leaders.
Eastenders stars roam these lanes
and byways and pop in here for a
quick one before (or after) their
rendezvous with Albert Square.

Coronet

338-346 Holloway Road N7
Tel: 0171 609 5014

A battery of swing doors usher you
into a vast foyer. From a gallery faces
from long-gone film posters stare
down. Then it all clicks. This is not a
pub, it's a cinema! JD Wetherspoon
have turned what used to be a picture
palace into a gin palace - well, more of
a beer hall. As you enter the
auditorium you half expect to be
greeted by a torch-wielding usherette
not a barman. From the gods (the
balcony) the stars look down. A giant
image of Bogart is mouthing "play it
again Sam" next to Cagney who is
probably thinking of sneering "You
dirty rat". A dancing Gene Kelly rubs
shoulders with Greta Garbo who just
wants to be alone. There is a replica of
a film producer centre stage. On the
walls are potted histories of the
movies. We are mere extras in this
celestial company. The ghost of Cecil B
DeMille that doyen of the biblical epic
seems to hover megaphone in hand
"Okay guys, it's a rap. The drinks are
on me." The drinks are reasonably
priced here.

The Country Pub in London

52 Cambridge Street SW1
Tel: 0171 834 5281

Once a working man's pub but now
stylishly refurbished as an elegant
country pub in the midst of the
hustle and bustle of Victoria and
Pimlico life. Excellent food and drink
can be had at reasonable prices. The
menu is wonderfully diverse and
includes giant Yorkshire Pudding with
sausages, fresh lobster and ginger
soup. Towards the end of the evening
the voices of the yuppie regulars seem
to get louder and louder and if you
keep your ear to the ground you may
pick up a valuable stock market tip.

The Cow

89 Westbourne Park Road
Royal Oak W2
Tel: 0171 221 0021

Over the road from the Westbourne
you will encounter The Cow.
A strange name perhaps?
Wouldn't Bull or Fox or even
Ferret be more macho? The Cow is an
example of how every name has a
history. In days of yore thirsty farmers
would pile into the 'Railway Tavern'
after a hectic day unloading their
cattle from the nearby railway.
Londoners being forever fond of an
apt nickname dubbed it the Cowshed.
A free house with a wide selection of
wines and specialist beers. Beware the
huge mural on the wall. It features
lobsters in hunting jackets riding
giant fish. After a few pints of their
Guinness this wildly surreal
extravaganza seems real. The Cow
combines the best of English, Irish
and Dutch hostelries where food and
drink complement each other.

Crockers

24 Aberdeen Place Maida Vale W9
Tel: 0171 286 6608

As you enter, be prepared to be mugged by a riot of marble and ornate furnishings. A feast for the taste buds as well as the eyes. Why this grandeur in a dull back street? The sad story goes that builder Frank Crocker thought Marylebone station was going to be built nearby. Nicknamed Crocker's Folly by the locals it ruined him financially and Crocker leapt to his death from the roof of his proud creation. It is rumoured that his ghost still haunts the site.

The Crown

43 Clerkenwell Green,
Clerkenwell has always been very historical. Now it is very fashionable with redundant offices and warehouses being converted into bijou apartments. From the Crown on Clerkenwell Green you can see the Middlesex Sessions House of Oliver Twist fame and the Karl Marx Memorial Library. The original well the Clerk fell into is but one minutes walk away as is the House of Correction not an establishment housing lewd ladies with whips but a recently renovated subterranean prison. The mediaeval city gate of Saint John of Jerusalem is a stone's throw away, The Crown is a Nicholson's pub with elegant Victorian features. During the summer, drinkers sit out on the Green (actually paving stones) and soak up the sun and there are no tall buildings to cast gloomy shadows.

The Dove

19 Upper Mall Hammersmith W6
Tel: 0181 748 5405

A 17th century inn overlooking the

bridge. This has been described as one of the best-loved riverside taverns in London town, and it is strikingly obvious why. It has countless literary and historical associations. The poet James Thomson wrote 'Rule Britannia' in an upper room and Charles II and Nell Gwynne drank at the inn together. Today, one of the kings of rock sometimes sups here. The stone terrace affords wonderful views of the Thames and its leafy banks.

The Eagle
Farringdon Road EC1
Tel: 0171 837 1353
This free house, situated close to the Guardian newspaper offices, always seems to be full of a merry throng of youngish professional people chatting nineteen to the dozen. What attracts them could be the food which has strong Mediterranean influences and is cooked at the bar in full view of the curious customer. You could almost graduate as a chef if you came here often enough.

Filthy McNasty & The Whiskey Cafe
68 Amwell Street EC1
Tel: 0171 837 8910
An island of traditional Irishness in village Islington. A massive silhouette of what looks like Sandemans Don crossed with Emilio Zapata eying up a particularly choice whiskey adorns the outside wall. Why an Hispanic? Well, for some obscure reason this bar is Mexican-Irish. The real 'Filthy M' was a hero of B movies who died of the demon drink. This intimate bar prides itself on a very wide selection of Irish whiskeys including Jamesons, Paddy and Powers. Of a Sunday morning you could sample a traditional Irish breakfast served between 12noon and 3pm, or Irish music most nights when much of the illumination comes from guttering candles in bottles. On the wall is a frieze of an Irish monk from the Book of Kells juxtaposed with a Mexican deity.

Flyman and Firkin
166-70 Shaftesbury Avenue WC2
Tel: 0171 240 7109
What's a flyman? He is the bloke who manipulates the scenery in a theatre. Theatrical paraphernalia festoon this vast cavernous pub. A life-size flyman hovers over you and a rain machine menaces you in the corner. There is a beer machine in the cellar; for this is a Firkin where they brew their ales on the spot. One of their 'best-sellers', Critic's Ale, although tasty is not quite strong enough to disarm a critic in my opinion. A better bet is Dogbolter which will render him legless - and might make him run and run and run - if he has too much. You have to tread the boards here - it seems the Firkins have a downer on carpets - and when you pay a visit to the 'actors' or 'actresses' (the loo) a sign says; 'Please adjust your fly as you are leaving the grid'.' This has proved to be one of the most popular of all Firkins. It is full most nights with crowds of youngish people attracted by the loudish music.

The French
49 Dean Street Soho W1
Tel: 0171 437 2477
Shrine to many artists and
bohemians. Francis Bacon was a
regular, and you can see where he got
some of the ideas for his
portraits from. The French
connection goes back to the last war
when this was a home to the Free
French. Only half pints of beer are
served in the bar - just as well, this is
a place to pose with a Pernod.

The George
77 Borough High Street.
Tel: 0171 407 2056
The only 17th century coaching inn
left in London. Leave your coach
outside as you enter the cobbled yard
and step back a few centuries. A
favourite of that gift to all landlords:
Charles Dickens.

The George
Great Portland Street W1
Tel: 0171 636 0863
Close to BBC in Langham Place, this
pub is also known as the Gluepot.
So-called by Henry Wood of "The
Proms' fame. His musicians
sometimes dallied too long in this
tavern and when they returned to the
Queen's Hall nearby a little bit
pizzicato, he accused them of staying
too long in "That bloody gluepot".
Very Victorian with original ceramics
and tiles.

The Grenadier
18 Wilton Row SW1
Tel: 0171 235 3074
The pub with a spook. The ghost is an
officer caught cheating at cards and
shot in the ensuing brawl, at a time
when the building was part of
Wellington's barracks. This tavern in
a mews is far from eerie though more
like a country ale house.

The Country House Pub in Pimlico

Hamilton Hall
Liverpool Street Station EC2
Tel: 0171 247 3579
As you enter this immense boozer be prepared to be transported to heaven by clusters of cheeky cherubs floating on cotton-wool clouds. The ceiling appears to be a mile high and is painted in rococo splendour. It is as if Rubens or Tiepolo popped in during their lunch hour to do a bit of dabbing with their tippling.
This listed building used to be the ballroom of the Great Eastern Hotel but the people who waltz in here these days are mainly City types.

The Holly Bush
Holly Mount off Heath Street.
Hampstead NW3
An old village pub that has the air of a bygone era about it. At least 18th century, for it was a favourite of that famous double act of Dr Johnson and James Boswell.

Hornimans
Hays Wharf Tooley Street EC1
Tel: 0171 407 3611
Formerly a Thameside warehouse. A spacious and attractively furnished place with a wide selection of beers. There are wonderful views of the Thames, The Tower, and Tower Bridge. The World War 11 heavy cruiser HMS Belfast is moored almost outside, but doesn't block the view. There are some great Thameside walks and The London Dungeon is nearby if the gruesome side of history appeals.

Island Queen
87 Noel Road N1
Tel: 0171 359 4037
Not so long ago a vast Margaret Thatcher hung suspended from the rafters of this pub. Not a bad fate but perhaps she frightened off the customers. So now she is replaced with life-sized pirates clambering over rigging. Far more user-friendly. Vast Victorian ornate mirrors and benches out front are other attractions of the pub, which lords it in a peaceful backwater of Islington. Regent's Canal is a stones throw away with its gaily painted barges. The whitewashed houses have the aspect of a Georgian village. In the 60's, a grisly murder shocked the neighbourhood. Joe Orton, the famous playwright who lived in Noel Road, was battered to death by his lover. He often popped into the Queen for a creme-de-menthe.

The King's Head
115 Upper St N1
Tel: 0171 226 1916

The doyen of theatre pubs and the first and probably the best. Back in the 70's it was Dan Crawford's vision, inspired by Brian McDermott, to turn the then scruffy Victorian boozer into a mini Old Vic. It weathered the storms and suffered the slings and arrows of outrageous fortune of years of a Philistine government,- and it's still going strong. Plays from this little theatre have ended up winning awards both in the West End and on Broadway. Buying a drink here comes with a surprise. The barman might say something like "That'll be £1.15 shillings, please" Shillings! Are we in Austria, Martha?" you can hear visitors saying. The till is caught in a time warp and has never heard of decimalisation. They not only cater for the theatrical muse but the musical muse as well and Bands play here 'till the wee hours.

The Lamb and Flag
33 Rose Street Covent Garden WC2
Tel: 0171 497 9504

Historic and literary connections. The poet Dryden was nearly done to death here by a group of thugs hired by the mistress of Charles II- a victim of his satire.

Lamb
94 Lambs Conduit Street. WC1
Tel: 0171 405 0713

Quaint and cosy Victorian pub in the heart of Bloomsbury. The group of that name were regulars - Virginia Woolf, Lytton Strachey, E.M. Forster - and it even has associations with

Robert Louis Stevenson and J.M. Barrie - the creator of Peter Pan. Brendan Behan used the upstairs room for poetry readings and Dylan Thomas was a regular. The bar does not possess a dead parrot but it does have 'snob screens'. These are ornate glass partitions which allow the drinker to see but not be seen.

Lord Moon of the Mall
76 Whitehall SW1
Tel: 0171 839 7701

A former Barclays Bank, now a J.D. Wetherspoon pub. The transformation from bank to bar is seamless. Although as you approach the marbled counter to buy a drink, you might get the impression you are making a with - drawal instead of investing in a pint. The decor is truly grandiose - like a St.James' club for gentlemen, with its antique paintings and comfortable armchairs This is the place for a civilised chat - perhaps about the past glories of the British Empire. There is an interesting story about the name Wetherspoon. The founder of this chain of pubs, Tim Martin, named them after a school teacher who told him, "You will never make anything of your life". There are now well over a hundred.

The Old Bank of England
194 Fleet Street EC4
Tel: 0171 430 2255

Formerly a branch of said bank replete with ornate ceiling, marble columns, chandeliers and striking murals of the bewigged directors of Fuller's Brewery.

Old King Lud
12 Ludgate Circus EC4
Tel: 0171 329 8517
Ludgate was the first gate into London when the city was surrounded by a stone wall and not just a ring of steel. Situated at the juncture of Fleet Street and Ludgate Hill which leads to St Paul's Cathedral this pub probably features the largest selection of cask ales in the metropolis - there's a minimum of twenty. Dark and cavernous, it has the feel of a mediaeval dungeon - which it was in the twelfth century. In the 16th century it went upmarket as it became the Lord Mayor's House.

The Pharaoh and Firkin
90 Fulham High Street SW10
Tel: 0171 731 0732
Enter the Valley of the Kings....in Fulham. I almost expected to be served by a mummy in this Firkin theme pub. It is true that the ancient Egyptians were the first to brew beer but I doubt if Rameses' local boozer was like this one. It is one vast cavern of a place resembling in size a hangar for airplanes. All around are Egyptian mementoes, artifacts and hieroglyphics that even Indiana Jones would find taxing to decipher. Come to think of it perhaps the Great Pyramid was built as a theme pub.

Phoenix and Firkin
5 Windsor Walk Denmark Hill SE5
Tel: 0171 701 8282
What's this? A pub in a station? Or is it a station in a pub? This totally original boozer has an Alice in Wonderland air of the surreal about it. A Bruce's pub that rose Phoenix-like from the ashes of a fire that gutted the British rail station it overlooks. There are large pews to sit on and newspapers for the customers to read. The walls are festooned with railway bric-a-brac. Try a very real ale called Dogbolter.

The Prince Bonaparte
80 Chepstow Road W2
Tel: 0171 229 5912
Formerly the Artesian. This was a popular pub with the boys in blue. Mainly the Flying Squad and Drug Squad who were working overtime. Nothing remains of those murky days. Friendly staff, wide selection of ales (a Bass House) and a wide open kitchen where you can watch your meal being cooked before your eyes. Their menu ranges from bangers and mash to Thai. Art Deco panelling has been retained from the old days.

The Prospect of Whitby
57 Wapping Wall E1
Tel: 0171 4811 1095
"Yo-ho-ho and a bottle of...Courage Best bitter, landlord please." This ancient seafarers tavern (built 1520) overlooks the Thames and takes its name from a ship that was formerly moored there. In days long gone, known as the Devil's Tavern, it was the haunt of pirates and sailors and, in the 16th century it became the execution site for these cutthroats. Captain Kidd himself was hung up in irons near here as a warning that crime does not pay. It paid handsomely for bloody Judge Jeffreys, the notorious 'hanging' judge. He used to sit in the tavern and watch the felons he had sentenced dangling from the gibbet - it no doubt gave him a wonderful appetite.

The Sherlock Holmes
10-11 Northumberland St WC2
Tel: 0171 930 2644
It is elementary to detect this pub:
just follow your nose down
Northumberland Avenue from
Trafalgar Square. This Victorian
edifice is a virtual museum to the
famed private eye of Baker Street.
There is a room of Holmesian
memorabilia, and photos of various
film and TV productions adorn the
walls. A veritable home from Holmes.

The Spaniards Inn
Spaniards Road, Hampstead NW3
Tel: 0181 455 3276
Dick Turpin the notorious highwayman, used to come here, sitting at an
upstairs window and observing
passing coaches to rob, no doubt
rehearsing his "your money or your
life" routine. What he would see now
would be the traffic bottleneck - the
only notorious feature today about
this ancient and historical inn.
Dickens set a scene from Pickwick
Papers in the rose garden. Lord
Byron was a regular and Keats was
inspired to write 'Ode to a
Nightingale' after observing the bird
here. The infamous Gordon rioters of
the 18th century were intent on
smashing up the nearby Kenwood
House but stopped off here for a swift
half. Most must have ended up
legless, for the army were called, and
after a fight, carried the remainder off
to Newgate where they were later
hanged. What better testimony to the
quality of their ales?

The Sherlock Holmes: A meeting place for followers of the great sleuth.

The Sun Inn
7 Church Road, Barnes

With its warren of tiny bars and nooks and crannies, its many levelled floor and sundry low ceilings it certainly eschews the straight line. Straight lines are de rigueur in the Barnes Bowling Club at the back of the Inn. Here, it is said Queen Elizabeth I was taught to play bowls by Drake. Well, you need a light break from sinking all those Spanish galleons don't you? This 18th century coaching inn is a treasure house of history and olde worde bric-a-brac, On a summer's day sit in the forecourt and admire the view. It's a picture postcard English village to perfection, dappled willow trees trail their fronds in Barnes Pond. A gang of Canada geese honk for supper. An airborne division of these geese flew within feet of me, one nearly nosediving into the pub sign. On top of all this the pub even has a ghost. He has it in for plates apparently. He bangs, moves or smashes them. Maybe he is the ghost of a Greek waiter.

Trafalgar Tavern
Park Row, SE10
Tel: 0181 858 2437

Glorious Greenwich, famed for its naval connections, the Maritime Museum, the Cutty Sark tea clipper, Francis Chichester's Gypsy Rose, the observatory and the Trafalgar Tavern. This magnificent Regency building looks for all the world like a ghostly white galleon about to set sail up the Thames. Dr Johnson, Thackeray and Dickens are just a few of the illustrious names to grace this elegant pub. Dr Crippen the murderer and Dick Turpin the highwayman also passed this way. Black Bess must have been a gem of a nag to have carried Turpin all the way from The Spaniard's Inn in Hampstead where he had his hideaway to Greenwich. Dickens set the wedding breakfast scene in 'Our Mutual Friend' here. Whitebait suppers are all the rage now - it is a recently revived tradition. On tap is a beer called Frigging in the Rigging. Sounds like a saucy line from a 'Carry On' film.

Tut n' Shive
235 Upper Street N1
Tel: 0171 359 7719

If you see Dracula standing at the bar imbibing a pint of vein rouge one might not have had one over the eight. This weird and wacky theme pub is like Hammer House of Horrors meets Marvel Comics. As you enter none other than Frankenstein's monster leers down at you. The walls are plastered with Horror magazines and children's comics and a WW1 Fokker plane is about to dive bomb a train which winds its way above the customers 'heads. My 'seat' was a bath tipped on its side. Immediately, thoughts of Haigh the Acid Bath murderer sprang to mind and I nipped into another seat - this time a coffin ! Welcome to the House of Fun.

The Warrington Hotel
93 Warrington Crescent W9
Tel: 0171 286 2929
More like a grandiose Victorian palace than a watering hole. Art Nouveau tiles rub shoulders with rude murals giving this establishment a somewhat Wildean feel. It used to be a brothel and so was owned by the Church of England.

Waterside Inn
82 York Way N1
Tel: 0171 837 7118
The water in question is the Regent's Canal and the inn is a warehouse cunningly disguised as an alehouse. Red brick outside, inside the inn is a riot of wood. Oak beams confront you wherever you look. The woodwork is genuine "ye olde" - it is taken from a Herefordshire barn, and there is a huge 17th century stone cider press in the centre of the bar. The terrace outside overlooks the canal.

The White Horse
Parson's Green SW6
Tel: 0171 736 2115
This pub on Parsons Green used to be a coaching inn. In 1837 the first women's cricket match was held on the Green. No doubt many maiden overs were bowled that day and the pub landlord provided them with tea. The decor today is comfortably unpretentious with its wooden floor and Chesterfield settees.A real grate fire is a rare and welcoming sight. The pub food is something to salivate over. There is venison in old roger and beef Casserole in Fuller's golden pride. Even the sausages are made with bass. You can also make your own potato crisps. It is not surprising that Sunday lunch can go on all day.

The rich exterior of the Salisbury Pub at 90 St Martin's Lane, in the heart of theatreland

Walkabout Inn

1 Henrietta Street WC2
Tel: 0171 379 5555

Even if you are down and out in
London, any ex-pat Aussie or Kiwi
should not back out of paying this
pub a visit. Or anyone else for that
matter who wants the genuine
flavour of down-under. Piped Kooka-
burra music, kangaroo steaks,
funnelweb spiders in the dunny. Not
really folks, but they tell me this is
the real McCoy, the sort of gaff
Crocodile Dundee might hang out in.
There's even a crocodile pinioned to
the wall - a rather cuddly, Disneyesque
kind of cobber. To make you feel even
more at home they show all the
major Australian and New Zealand
sporting events on large screens as
soon as they are flown over. They also
have music five nights a week.

The Westbourne

101 Westbourne Park Villas W2
Tel: 0171 221 1332
Open seven days a week.

Very popular with photographers,
artists, models, actors and musicians.
It's situated above the river Westbourne
which was dammed in the 19th
century to form the Serpentine Lake
in Hyde Park.

This is clearly another pub where the
food matters as much as the drink.
Amongst the brews are Dortmunder,
Union and Leffe. The latter is a
Belgian beer that packs a powerful
punch. A wide and spacious terrace
affords a view of the world walking by.

Ye Olde Cheshire Cheese

Wine Office Ct., 45 Fleet Street EC4
Tel: 0171 353 6170

The rich aroma of maggoty history
oozes from its every fibre. A real piece
of Old London. Food is not served in
the pub but you can dine in the
adjoining restaurant. Steak and
kidney pie is a long time favourite
and game pudding is served during
the winter months. Dr Johnson would
be at home here even today. He lived
just around the corner in Gough
Square.

The Westbourne: Where food matters as much as drink.

Pubs with Striptease

Pubs with striptease do not always tell you from the outside what to expect. Often, but not always, there are signs indicating exotic dancing. It is just another term for striptease in a pub. Exotic, however. are the countries of origin of the girls who take off their clothes: admission is generally free (except where otherwise indicated) and the girls earn their money by 'whiprounds' before each dance.

Although there are no hard and fast rules as to how much you should give them, anything less than 50 pence is considered impolite. £1 would be more appropriate. Drinks are charged at normal Central London prices.

The Crown and Shuttle
223 Shoreditch High Street. E1
Mon -Fri: 1pm-3pm and 5.30pm-11pm
Beer: Murphy's.

Shoreditch is the part of London with the largest number of pubs with striptease. Coming from Liverpool Street station soon after reaching Shoreditch High Street you can find this pub on your left-hand side. In the space of a shoe box two strippers . usually recline on a pool table put to better use.

The Norfolk Village
Shoreditch High Street E1
Beer: Guinness, Adnams.
Music: DJ
Carrying on on the left-hand side you pass a Majestic Wine Warehouse to reach this pub. Between two and three girls strip on or in front of a small stage at the rear end of the pub. Between their acts they tend to sit on the bar. One of the few strip pubs to attract a fair number of female drinkers, usually sitting near the front door.

The White Horse
64 Shoreditch High Street E1
Tel: 0171 739 3702
1pm 3pm (daily except Sats)
and 5.30pm -11p.m.
Four different strippers
Beers: Guinness, Adnams.
Opposite on the right hand side this pub claims to be on the site of a former hostelry opened in 1462 and presumes no lesser man than Shakespeare amongst its regulars - this is probably questionable, although on Shoreditch High Street you find St. Leonard's Church whose graveyard houses the remains of many actors from Shakespeare's theatre troupe. Food counter open at lunchtime. A DJ does the music.

The Rainbow Sports Bar

Shoreditch High Street E1
Tel: 0171 739 2959
Beers: Guinness, London Pride, Bass
This pub is an absolute must. It has
been refurbished and opened under
its present name in 1998. The
neonlights outside show you the way
and are visible from afar. Between
1pm and midnight (11.30pm. on a
Sunday) six to eight girls offer non-
stop striptease on an elevated stage
with poles and mirrors. You can sit
close to the stage on non-removable
bar stools. As the note says inside 'Ask
your favourite girl' and for a tenner
she will do you a table dance in
another corner of this small but
compact venue. This pub comes
nearest to the atmosphere of a table
dance club. While the stripping goes on
Sky Sports is being shown. Avoid
during major sports events. The
evening girls start stripping at 7pm.

Browns

1 Hackney Road E2.
Tel: 0171 739 4653
Beers: Guinness, Tetley's (Creamflow
version and Real Cask-conditioned)
Further on, this large pub is impossible
to miss. Do not be put off by the door -
men, who will only stop you if you
wear trainers. About four ladies at
any one time strip on a large elevated
stage with mirrors and poles with the
men standing in front of it. Occasionally
two girls strip in tandem. For a
private dance book at the bar (£10 in
a separate private cabin). At the rear
end you can play pool billiards, if you
that is if you feel you can ignore the
beauties. Erotic drawings decorate
the wall near the stage.DJ.

The Spread Eagle

Kingsland Road E8
This pub reopened its doors in 1998
after a long period of closure. In the
excitement of it all the management
forgot to install a heating system. But
that has now been 'sorted', when they
realised that stripping at arctic
temperatures is not profitable. The
two to three girls do not only use the
stage but the entire pub and strip in
your face.

Ye Olde Axe

69 Hackney Road
Tel: 0171 729 5137
Beers: Beamish; Courage
This sister pub of The Spread Eagle
could do with a little aesthetic
uplifting outside. The word 'striptease'
is meant to shine in neonlight.
Unfortunately the letters TEA have
not been illuminated for a very long
time, which gives an unpleasant
impression. Most of the strippers
ignore the stage and come round to
strip in your face. You can frequently
see them reclining in all their natural
beauty right on the floor of the pub. If
you ask nicely, some might even play
pool billiard with you. Expect to pay
£2 admission charge on at the
weekend but in return the stripping
goes on until 2am.

The Seven Stars

Brick lane E1
Tel: 0171 426 0135
Mon-Sat between 7pm-11pm.
Two girls strip for your pleasure. Not
all customers seem to appreciate this,
as it is a common practice to play pool
billiard just in front of the stage,
which severely restricts ones view.

The management are unwilling to interfere, and as a form of compromise have stopped the girls from reclining on the billiard table instead. Expect long breaks between the acts. They still manage to maintain the image of a family pub with a fair number of female customers. Perhaps that is the reason why there is no indication outside to tell you that striptease is going on inside.

The Nag's Head
17 Whilechapel Road El
Tel: 0171 377 8005
Mon-Fri 1pm-3pm and 5.30pm-11pm.
Between two and three girls strip on an elevated stage. During the breaks you may admire the erotic drawings in the pub. When I asked for it, the Kebab service had been discontinued.

The Ten Bells
84 Commercial Street Whitechapel E1
Tel: 0171 377 2145
1pm-3pm weekdays; 5.30pm-8pm Tuesday, Wednesday and Friday
This is a real find. In the heart of Jack the Ripper land is this seedy piece of Victoriana. The Ripper stalked these streets and may have used this pub. The pub has the air of having never changed since those days with its basic bare boards and wrought iron tables and some magnificent tiled panoramas of Spitalfields market which adorn one of the walls. Walk in here any week- day lunchtime and you are in for a big surprise. As soon as I opened the door I was greeted by

a naked lady writhing exotically to the music. The Ten Bells was known for many years as the 'Jack the Ripper' and seeing these girls strut their stuff on this tiny stage in the middle of the floor, which they never leave, these dancers give show business a new dimension. Signs indicating exotic dancing can only be seen when there are strippers in the pub. For the rest of the time the pub cultivates the image of being a respectable stop-off on the tourist trail.

The Lord Nelson
17 Mora St, EC 1
Tel: 0171 253 6389
Mon-Sat: Two girls stripping between 1pm-3pm and 7pm-11pm
Near Moorfields Eye Hospital, but a little tucked away from City Road is this fairly spacious pub offering striptease six days a week..

Keen admirers of the female anatomy

The Griffin

125 Clerkenwell Road EC1

0171 405 3855

Mon-Fri:Stripping between 1pm- 2pm.
Bass:Guinness.Tetley's (Creamflow
and Cask-conditioned) Food

In London's legal quarter in Gray's
Inn is the sister pub to Browns.
Expect to see the same girls. Private
dances (in a cabin) may be booked for
£10 at the bar. I wonder, however, how
many customers enjoy having their
name shouted across the rather small
pub by the DJ when their chosen girl
is ready for them for a private show.

The Flying Scotsman

Caledonian Road N1

Beers: Guinness

This pub always looks like being in
need of serious dry cleaning. The more
surprising that the gents can now be
visited without any danger of getting
wet feet. But then again, the rough
image may have its appeal. Between
two and four girls-(more as the
evening progresses) -enchant a
usually packed house. That may
explain why the sign outside
indicating exotic dancers has
disappeared. Very popular on
Saturdays with rugby and football fans
before returning home to destinations
outside London. If you like to sit down
while watching your strippers, this
pub is probably not for you.

The Windsor Castle

309 Harrow Road W9

Tel: 0171 289 7039

The stripping is now confined to 7pm.

on Thursday, Fridays and Saturdays
and takes place in an upstairs bar
with a separate entrance. At the door
they charge you £2 "for the young
lady". but there are no whiprounds.
You are better off watching striptease
elsewhere. I felt sorry for the girl who
was on when I visited and when I saw
her the following week elsewhere the
views on offer were so much more
enchanting. Just goes to show, you pay
for what you get.

The Queen Anne

139 Vauxhall Walk SE1

Tel: 0171 735 2079

Between 12noon.and 12 midnight.
Two girls are on at any one time for
three hours

From the outside the pub gives the
impression of having been shut down
for at least ten years without anyone
ever having dared to go inside again.
The first dance is topless only with no
prior whiround. The stage is attached
to a little catwalk where you can sit
close-up and watch every detail. With
the right barman on (not Wednesdays)
you always feel assured of the best
Guinness in London. He certainly
takes his time to serve it to the
highest standard.

The Barley Mow

The New Covent Garden SW8.

Tel: 0171 726 5555

Still in Vauxhall is this trader's pub
inside London's main fruit and veg
market with very early opening hours.
For the striptease you have to wait
until Friday and Saturday lunchtime.

Clubbing

The London nightclub scene has long been recognised as one of the most fast-moving and colourful in the world. Ever since the 50's, the creative self-expression of the city has fostered a culture of music and fashion whose energy permeates all types of dance hall. Whatever your taste in music, if you can tap your toes to it, you're sure to find a dance floor on which to 'bop your body' to it too!

London's clubs can loosely be split into three groups: the mainstream, the cosmopolitan and the trendy. Of these, the first are by far the most popular, patronised by a broad cross-section of the partying public, from Brylcreem boys to businessmen. Because of this melting pot effect, and the impersonality that such cavernous venues sometimes have, the atmosphere is always very jolly with everyone clubbing together to enjoy a great night out.

The largest in London, indeed in Europe, is Equinox, whose palatial exterior has at last given a shine to shabby Leicester Square. It claims to hold 2,000 people and has a dance floor and lighting rig which make up for in magnitude what they lack in imagination. As such, it has to be the least fashionable nightspot in the West End, sharing the spirit, if not the size, that characterises so many of England's regional clubs. But such a lack of pretension is, of course, its main attraction. It's also interesting to note that Equinox seems to enjoy a greater balance between the sexes than its competitors. For those familiar with a dance floors crowded with blokes this might come as a welcome relief.

...ing the night away

If ever a venue was tailor-made for the gossip columns it has to be Stringfellows. Its intimacy and opulent sophistication attract an older and more wealthy customer, from Windsor princesses to soap opera queens, but the music remains chart-based and spritely. If you fancy a romantic interval between dances there's a sumptuous bar and dining area to escape to, with cosy lighting and attractive flower arrangements. If, however your appetite is whetted by an unconventional mixture of music and design you're sure to be satisfied by the fashionable venues London has to offer, although some are much less accommodating than others. The Wag on Wardour Street, for instance, congratulates itself on being the most elite night spot in town and as such is patronised by those who deem themselves so superior that it's social suicide for them to glance at anyone else. Far more agreeable are the Ministry of Sound at The Elephant and Castle and the Camden Palace, north of the West End on Camden High Street, which are each unique, but not exclusive. The Palace owes its flamboyant extravagance to the New Romantic era of pop music in the early 80's when stars were apt to dress as modern-day pirates and fops. An emporium of colourful levels and video screens, it also has a large stage, cocktail bars and a restaurant.

One-night discos are still a popular feature of such clubs, when a non-resident DJ steals the control deck to pump out his (or her) own variety of music. The 'Wednesday Night' is always well attended at the Palace with its infectious selection of 60's soul and R'n'B hits.

With such a diversity of clubs you can hardly go wrong. So go on, give your feet a treat. They might regret the blisters but you'll not regret the night.

The Limelight: Rave-worshippers at the converted church in Shaftesbury Avenue W1

Clubbing

Please take note: London's club scene is very diverse and constantly changing. The following is a small selection of some of the best and/ or more established venues. For entrance fee, dress code and up to date information, telephone your choice *before setting out.*

Contemporary

Bar Rumba
36 Shaftesbury Avenue W1
U: Piccadilly Circus
Tel: 0171 287 2715
A daytime tapas bar with various club nights. Soulful Garage and House with some rare groove thrown in for a mixed laid-back start to the week's groove.

Bagley's
Kings X Freight Depot York Way N1
Tel: 0171 278 2777
This club has a major overhaul in the last year. Freedom is London's first 'freestyle' night all in one playing popular house, techno, American garage, and 60's classics with a very good sound system.

Blue Note
1 Hoxton Square N1
Tel: 0171 729 8440
Quite a laid-back atmosphere. The venue is on one floor but three levels, with plenty of seating all round. Regularly plays host to a number of styles including techno, reggae, jazz funk and lots, lots more.

Night clubbers

Gass Club
Whitcomb Street SW1
Tel: 0171 839 3922
One Night Stand: Matt Lamont, Karl Brown and Norris Windross play upfront, underground garage. Unremarkable mid-size venue. Smart and sociable late-20's crowd.

Grays
4 Grays Inn Road WC1
Tel: 0171 430 1161
Some hip-hop, some rap, some soul, no garage and everything funky for a sociable twenty-and thirty-something crowd. Busy.

Contemporary

Iceni
11 White Horse Street W1
Tel: 0171 495 5333
Funk to jazz to hip-hop on two
different levels, plus jam session,
short films in the coffee bar, and
board games in the third floor
chill-out lounge.

Limelight
136 Shaftesbury Avenue W1
Tel: 0171 434 0572
Fri & Sat:10.30pm-3.30am
Spectacular surroundings in a
former church, 70ft. dome over the
main dance floor and numerous bars/
lounges. Goes through phases in its
popularity and doesn't seem to be in
one of them at the moment.

Stacey Young and Tamara Beckwith :
enjoying a girls night out

Maximus
14 Leicester Square WC2
Tel: 0171 734 4111
10.30pm-3.30am
'Mrs Wood's Big Night Out' is the
popular night here with a mix of
techno, hard and handbag house to
techno babe. Mostly hip and
happening crowd and that can
include several wannabes (and a few
neverwillbes).

The Rock Garden
The Piazza, Covent Garden WC2
Tel: 0171 836 4052
Fri:11pm-5am (check other times)
'This is one of the more established
venues for 'one nighters'. Friday and
Saturday soul/funk/garage and swing.

Ministry of Sound
103 Gaunt Street
Elephant and Castle SE1
Tel: 0171 378 6528
Fri: 12pm-8am Sat: 12pm-9am
Huge warehouse style club with
possibly the best sound system in the
country. Vast dark dance floor, huge
bar (no alcohol but psycho-active
cocktails). Cinema and VIP chill-out
lounge. Prepare to queue.

Subterania
12 Acklam Road
Ladbroke Grove W10
Tel: 0181 960 4590
10.30pm-3.30 am
Loud and funky essential grooves
(jazz, swing and soul) plus live dance
music. West Side story-inspired decor.
Youngish crowd.

Bar Madrid
4 Winsley Street W1
Tel: 0171 436 4650
Mon-Sat 5pm-3am; Sun 7.30pm-12
Lively Latin tapas bar, restaurant and
nightclub with live music and
entertainment and dance classes of
Lambada; Samba-Reggae; Real Salsa
and Salsa school.

Cafe de Paris
3 Coventry Street Piccadilly W1
Tel: 0171 734 7700
Glam revamped venue in the heart of
Piccadilly. Dress as wild as you dare!
Also plays host to private parties,
various one-off events and The Brit
Awards.

Wag Club
35 Wardour Street W1
Tel: 0171 437 5534
Open 10pm-5am
Unpretentious atmosphere attracting
a sharp and interesting crowd. House,
garage and world groove downstairs,
rap and rare groove upstairs.

Camden Palace
1a Camden Road
Camden Town NW1
Tel: 0171 387 0428
Tue-Sat 8pm-3am
Renovated multi-level theatre.
Tue: Indie-rock night with live bands.
Mon : Thurs and Sun
'one nighters,' private promoters.

Crazy Larry's
533 Kings Road SW10
Tel: 0171 376 5555
Open Fri-Sat 10.30pm- 3am
Cosy nightclub in the heart of
Chelsea, with relaxed atmosphere and
cosmopolitan clientele.

Electric Ballroom
184 Camden High Street NW1
Tel: 0171 485 9006
London's biggest rock, gothic, punk
and heavy metal night on Saturday.
Popular unpretentious club playing
anything from hip hop to house to
indie downstairs, jazz and R&B
upstairs.

The promoter and the party people

Mainstream

Equinox
Leicester Square WC2
Tel: 0171 437 1446
Tues-Sat 9pm-3.30am.
Enormous 'disco-tec' playing
commercial dance music to a crowd
that includes tourists and office girls.

Hippodrome
Cranbourne Street Leicester Square W1
Tel: 0171 437 4311
Well-established, huge, glitzy and
very commercial club, with an
impressive light and laser show and
podium dancers. Mainstream dance
music. Guest PA's on Friday nights.

Los Locos Beachclub
14 Soho Street W1
Tel: 0171 287 0005
Tue-Sat 5pm-3am
Los Locos Tejas
24 Russell Street WC2
Tel: 0171 379 0220
Mon-Sat from 5pm until 3am
Happy hour is Tuesday (all night)
with 50% off all drinks. Guest Fun
Mexican eatery with tiled floors,
wooden tables and colourful wall
paintings, that turns into a loud and
lively club later in the evening. Set
party menu.

Mambo Inn
Loughborough Street SW9
Tel: 0171 737 2943
Fri and Sat only 10pm-2am
Funky mix of Latin, African and
jazz, for a very diverse crowd and
are relaxed house-party type
atmosphere.

Top model Claudia Schiffer - goes out on
the town.

St Moritz Club
159 Wardour Street W1
Tel: 0171 437 0525
Open:Mon-Sat 9pm-3am.
This deceptively spacious cellar has
played host to various changes in the
music culture over the years and is
continually reinventing itself. Well
worth checking out.

Strawberry Moons
15 Heddon Street Piccadilly W1
Tel: 0171 437 7300
Capacity for up to 500 customers
Open Mon-Wed 5pm-11pm; Thu-Sat
5pm-3am
A lively bar and restaurant in the
heart of Piccadilly just off Regent
Street. It fuses the showmanship of
P.T. Barnum the mystery of Harry
Houdini and the grandeur of Ziegfeld
Follies, all this combined with a great
atmosphere good food and slick
service, seems to be the perfect recipe
for a great night out.

Please take note: London's club scene is very diverse and constantly changing. The following is a small selection of some of the best and/ or more established venues. For entrance fee, dress code and up to date information, telephone your choice *before setting out.*

Stringfellows
16 Upper St. Martin's Lane WC2
Tel: 0171 240 5534
Open Mon-Sat 8pm-3am.
Well-known disco with three bars and a restaurant and now also the home of 'Cabaret of Angels' the table-side dancing sensation.(Check nights) The club is now in its 19th year and Peter 'Pan' Stringfellow is still as enthusiastic as ever. This is still the place where the minor celebs, soap opera stars still meet and greet, although nowadays it's alongside suburban office girls on their big night out. (Smart dress.)

Madame Jojo's
8-10 Brewer Street W1
Tel: 0171 734 2473
Thu, Fri and Sat 10pm-3am
Sunday Night is Funk Night
Entrance £20, £17.50 seating; or £12.50 standing
The latest show to hit this intimate cabaret bar is entitled 'Return to Planet Jo Jo', inspired by Star Wars and Barbarella with two beefy bikers thrown in for good measure. The biggest and most glittered drag cabaret show to date features Purdy and the Barbettes, and forms the most glamourous chorus line in Soho. The extremely diverse clientele includes, West End actors, tourists and Essex boys.

The Green Room at the Café Royal
68 Regent Street Piccadilly Circus W1
Tel: 0171 437 9090
Open:Wed-Sat for dinner/cabaret from 8.pm; Cabaret at 9.30pm
Dancing between 11.30 and 3am
This 'Green Room' is now pretty well established as a top cabaret venue, attracting all the big names on the cabaret circuit. The room can seat around 160 comfortably having gone through major refurbishment in the last year. The set price a la carte menu, including the show is £45 (depending on the performer) and it's worth every Euro.

Indigo at Madame Jojo's

Ruby's Dance Club
49 Carnaby Street W1
Tel: 0171 287 3957
Open Mon-Sun from 12noon-10pm
This is one of the longest running
dance clubs in London. Here, you can
be taught Ballroom, Jive and Latin
dancing and you don't have to bring a
partner. The music is everything from
Abba to T. Rex but bring your own
alcohol as the club has a restricted
license.

Talk of London
Parker Street, Drury Lane WC2
Tel: 0171 405 1516
Open Mon-Sat 7.30pm until late.
Cost: £37.50 inclusive
Just off Drury Lane and next to the
theatre that Cats have occupied since
it opened, is this cabaret and floor
show. The standard male vocal and
girl dancers provide the main cabaret

Showtime at the **Talk of London**

and the price also includes, a resident
band, a speciality act and a
four - course meal. This form of
entertainment seems to be very
popular with the people that make up
television audiences during the
recording of quiz-shows.

Las Estrellas
2 Inverness Mews Off Queensway W2
Tel: 0171 221 5038
Doors open 9.15pm Entrance £10
Tuesdays and Saturday between
9.30pm-1am are Tango nights;
Every Wednesday is: Russian Music
night. For other nights phone the
above number. One of the best Tango
clubs around with beautiful Spanish
ornamental decoration, white painted
walls and dark wooden tables. Full
bar and tapas. Cabaret comes to
Bayswater with West End performers
Tango Argentine classes & Tango
Dancing.

Caesar's
156 160 Streatham Hill SW2
Tel: 0181-671 3000
Open to 4am
Venue with Roman style decor and
costumes, murals of Roman scenes,
statues and columns, marble,
ornamental cornices and Roman
artefacts, The a la carte menu
includes vegetarian choices. Resident
twelve piece orchestra, cabaret acts,
singer compere, singers, dance troupe
and resident DJ. The sound and light
engineers provide a spectacular show
Adjoining is Caesar's is the Forum a
membership only nightclub that
caters for the over twenty five age
group.

Dance/Cabaret

K-Bar Chelsea
266a Fulham Road SW10
Tel: 0171 352 6200
Tue-Sat 8.30pm-2am.
The latest sounds in Salsa from
South America, with star dancers.
Classes from 8pm.Private members
bar with a very fashionable crowd.

Tiroler Hut
27 Westbourne Grove W2
Tel: 0171 727 3981
Open Mon-Sat 8.30pm-4am
'The only cow bell cabaret show in the
country.' Is the proud boast of
lederhosen - clad- owner, Joseph
Friedman. Joseph has been providing
good food and music since 1967. He
plays the accordion, along with other
instruments, with a genuine
enthusiasm. And like all good
entertainers he likes to leave his
audience at the end of an evening
wanting more. A fun place to let it all
hang-out.

Sarastro Restaurant
126 Drury Lane WC2
Tel: 0171 836 0101
Open seven days a week from 12noon-
12midnight .
Sunday: Various Musicians perform.
Opera Nights every Monday
Ten 'private boxes' with seating
facilities for two up to fourteen
This restaurant is a great find. Hidden
away behind a modest entrance in the
residential section of Drury Lane and
within a roar of the Royal Opera
House - you will discover Sarastro. The
atmosphere is bustling and very
theatrical. Boxes surround the main
restaurant so you can observe the
proceedings down below whilst feeling
totally snug and private. The food on
offer is Mediterranean with a strong
Turkish influence; it's reasonably
priced and very adequate. Even if you
don't like opera, or music - you will
simply adore your dining experience at
this unique restaurant.

Showtime at **Sarastro Restaurant** in Drury Lane

Hostess Clubs

Casanova
181 Edgware Road Sussex Gardens
London W2
This part of London is known to the natives as, 'downtown Dubai' The reception you get on arrival at the Casanova is warm and friendly and the hostesses are generally attractive and the drinks cheaper than similar West End clubs. The main entertainment comprises of 'Karaoke' with the customers entertaining the customers and on one pretty dire evening the hostesses entertaining the hostesses. A floor - show in the shape of a belly dancer interrupts some horrendous renditions of classic recordings.

Crazy Horse
199 Swallow Street W1
Tel: 0171 734 6666
Swallow Street seems to be isolating itself from the rest of Soho, and in this small cosy little Street off Regent Street, you will find the Crazy Horse. This time offering us a new form of erotic cabaret described as 'lingerie dancing' as the main attraction.

Directors Lodge
13 Mason's Yard SW1
Tel: 0171 930 2540
Open Mon-Fri 9pm -3am
Live resident band and cabaret acts throughout the evening and a licensed restaurant serving Thai food. Dancing and dining companions are available and always seem to be close at hand.

Masters Club
12Denman St Piccadilly Circus W1
Open Mon-Fri 4pm-3.00am
Tel: 0171 734 4243
Non-members:£10
A discreet drinking/hostess club in the heart of Soho. The management are quick to point out that you do not have to pay a hostess fee and they have no hidden extras. Despite the club like atmosphere it is also open to non-members by coughing-up £10 on the door.

Miranda Club and Restaurant
9 Kingley Street West Soho W1
Tel: 0171 437 6695
Mon-Fri 9pm-3am
This slightly dated club occupies a spacious, but intimate basement, just off Carnaby Street in West Soho. A full a la carte menu is on offer, and cabaret in the form of striptease. Hostesses are available if you need a dining companion or if you decide to dance to their five-piece orchestra.

The New Churchills
52 Piccadilly W1
Tel: 0171 408 0226
Continuous erotic cabaret and floor show from10.30pm Lapdancing has now been added to what the owners describe as 'entertainment

New Gaslight
4 Duke of York Street.
Off Jermyn Street SW1
Tel: 0171 930 8050
Open: Mon-Fri 9pm-2am
The New Gaslight has undergone various changes over the years and has now reverted back once again - to being a good old-fashioned hostess club. Under the new management scheme of things table-dancing has been introduced with dining companions available, only if required.

New Georgian Club
4 Mill Street W1.
Tel: 0171 629 2042
Open Mon-Sat 10pm - 3am
This small and intimate club has been established for a great many years and is located on the West side of Soho. A varied cabaret act is usually part of the entertainment with dining companions standing by to converse or dine with you.

The Stork Club
99 Regent Street,W1
Tel: 0171 734 3686/1393
Open Mon-Sat 8.30pm-4am
A cosy club, a few yards from the 'dilly'. Excellently choreographed floorshows changing twice nightly at 11.30pm and 1am. Dine from the à la carte menu, or watch the show from the cocktail bar while you drink.

Toppers
61 Poland Street W1
Tel: 0171 439 9819
Open Mon-Fri 6.30pm -3am

McCoy's

BRITISH MASSAGE PARLOUR GUIDE

Please send me by return of post your complete guide to
MASSAGE PARLOURS IN THE UK,
and I enclose my cheque, postal order for £10.00 (to include postage and packing.)

Name...

Address...

....

....**Post code**..........................

Cheques and postal orders payable to:Niche Publications Limited

Niche Publications

P.O. Box 20988

31 London Street, London W2 3GX

Striptease Clubs

The Sunset Strip
30 Dean Street Soho W1
Tel: 0171 437 7229
Established 1958
Admission £12.50 with no time limit.
Open: Mon-Sat 12noon-1am
Sun 3pm-10pm
Some major changes have taken
place since our last visit to this long -
- established club and it has
undergone serious refurbishment
under the new management team.
The new owners tell us they want to
bring the tease back into strip. The
sleaze aspect seems to have
disappeared now that the middle
Englanders have finally discovered
striptease via lap-dancing. Here you
can watch around eight girls
performing in rota, for a compact and
enthusiastic audience, for as little as
the entrance fee.

Boulevard Striptease
7-12 Walkers Court Soho W1
Tel: 0171 734 5103
Mon -Thu 12noon -11pm; Fri & Sat
12noon-12.midnight. Sun 1pm-10pm.
Continuous performances with up to
6 dancers in rota. Bar. All day
re-admission £12.50, no time limit
This is a fully licensed strip club
where your admission ticket lasts all
day and punters can come (and go) at
will. The club is keen to point out that
no extra charges are involved, but if
you wish to 'tip' the performers I am
sure it would be appreciated.

The Carnival
12 Old Compton Street Soho W1
Tel:0171 437 8337
'This is a respectable establishment'
the management are keen to point out
on a cardboard print out. But if it is
that respectable why should they need
to point it out? Former page three girls
decorate the reception area giving the
impression that this is what is on
offer inside. Untrue.

Raymond's Revuebar
2 Walker's Court. Brewer Street W I
Tel: 0171 734 1593
Admission £25, £20, and £10.
Two performances of Exotica 2000
Mon to Sat 8pm and 10pm.
The so-called festival of erotica has
been the formula that has worked well
for Paul 'Striptease' Raymond for
around 40 years, but more recently
have had stiffer competition from the
lap dancing venues. Located in the
heart of the seediest part of Soho.

SUNSET STRIP

30 Dean Street Soho W1
London's best striptease club
invites you to enjoy continuous
full striptease on stage including
double acts and fantasy shows:
teachers,nurses, bondage
secretaries,traffic wardens,etc.etc
Stunning show girls to entertain
you. Not to be missed.

Stag parties catered for.
Entrance ticket £12.50
(Valid all day) No hidden extras

Tel: 0171 437 7229

Private Members Clubs

Literally within staggering distance of Groucho's - but for people who want to drink, have a serious chat, and keep a low profile.

Colony Room Club
41 Dean Street W1
Tel: 0171 437 9179
Waiting list for membership
Halfway down Dean Street in the heart of Soho you will find one of London's most famous clubs.The small room with a bar down one side and walls painted emerald green and encrusted with dusty memorabilia has been the hideaway artists from Francis Bacon to Damien Hirst for a great many years. It is possibly the last in a dying breed of drinking clubs for the serious drinker. The club recently introduced a new bar-staffing system; once a month one of the celebrity members and partner have to run the bar, and serve the drinks.

Chelsea Arts
143 Old Church Street SW3
Tel: 0171 376 3311
Subscription: £200
Has a 2000 strong fairly mixed membership, in the 30-up age bracket. The members include mainly artists and graphic designers, but you need to be interviewed, proposed /seconded. Reasonably priced accom-modation and is open all year round.

Embargo
533b Kings Road SW10
Tel: 0171 351 5038.
Open Mon-Sat 8pm-3am
Annual Membership: £200

Annabels
44 Berkeley Square W1
Tel: 0171 629 2350
Annual Membership: £500
Joining fee: £250
Open: Mon-Sat 8pm-3am
Probably the most chic club in London with a membership that boasts royals, millionaires and people from the world of show business. In fact the club is so heavily endowed with celebrities you're inclined to feel you are the only person in the world that nobody has ever heard of. There is a six month waiting period to join but if you happen to know an existing member, this should help.

Blacks Private Club
67 Dean Street W1
Tel:0171 287 3381
Annual Membership: £200
Open: Mon-Sat 8am-midnight

This club is frequented by a very sophisticated Chelsea crowd as well as models, actors and thirtysomething City types. Modern/ European food and all-night breakfasts are served, with dance music during the week, and live jazz at the weekend.

The Groucho Club

45, Dean Street, W1
Tel: 0171 439 4685
 Annual Membership: £275
Joining fee: £100
With a strong emphasis on folk from the publishing world, mature TV producers/directors and the usual smattering of advertising executives with an attitude of 'let's get totally rat-arsed'. They have an eighteen month waiting list for new members.

International Sportsman's Club

63 Kensington High Street W8
Tel: 0171 937 3330
Annual membership: £280 `
Once owned by football supremo Terry Venables and known as Scribes. The new owners have completely revamped the entire club to make it what one of the directors called 'more Kensington' .

Mortons

28 Berkeley Square W1
Tel: 0171 408 2483
Annual Membership: £325
Joining fee: £100
With over five thousand members, this fashionable club is set in the style of the thirties and is very popular with the fortysomething crowd. The club has undergone considerable changes over the years and that famous 'piano' is now in the downstairs restaurant.

Soho House

40 Greek Street Soho W1
Tel: 0171 734 5188
Membership: £300 per year
Joining fee: £100
Open Seven days a week
Soho House is a haven for media moguls who prefer the understated approach. Presenting a distinct alternative to its neighbours Groucho's, Blacks and the Union Club. The club offers comfortable sofas, dark corners for low key meetings, and the kind of relaxed atmosphere that makes you feel at home rather than on show. It may be for this reason that the club attracts the kind of members that are the envy of its rivals. From Hugh Grant and Mick Jagger to Steve Coogan, Johnathan Ross et al - all seem to enjoy the chic anonymity of 'The House'. Among the other reasons are a first class restaurant run by the wonderful 'Podge', featuring modern European cuisine. A rooftop area for dining or drinking al fresco and private rooms for meetings or dinner parties. The membership 'waiting list' currently runs to around two years.

Tramp

40 Jermyn Street SW1
Tel: 0171 734 3174
£300 per annum
This club was once described by novelist Jackie Collins as 'an old whore' - always there, always ready for your demands and always prepared to give you a good time.

Tramp has been a favourite of the rich and famous for the past thirty years. Visiting celebs wanting to dance the night away wind up there sooner or later.

The Met Bar
Metropolitan Hotel
19 Old Park Lane W1
Tel: 0171 447 5757
Open:Mon-Thurs 9.30am- 3.pm
Fri-Sats 24 hours and Sun to 10.30pm
Now well established as one of London's most exclusive venues with a strict policy: they don't want it to turn into a knocking shop. If you do get in, you'd be forgiven for thinking that a rich businessman from a nearby hotel would be a good idea to help with the bill. A long night on your own credit card should be viewed with trepidation. Membership is required only after 6pm, so the bar is open to the hoi polloi for lunch and afternoon tea should you want to go in daylight hours to a place designed for nightlife. To be a member you must go to the hotel, fill out an application form, let them see the cut-of your jib, wait an unspecified period of months, and bingo! - you're in.

The Roof Garden
99 Kensington High Street W8.
Tel: 0171 937 7994
Open: Thu and Sat 8pm-3am
Members only club.
Non-members admitted at club's discretion if dining. Annual membership: £200
This is Richard Branson's extremely smart club/restaurant overlooking High Street Kensington. The exclusive rooftop rendezvous has a great garden setting, is 'grade 1 listed' and is open to the public each day between 9am and 5pm. In the evening you can listen to 'live jazz' over dinner followed by dancing.

The serene surroundings of the Roof Garden in Kensington

Club Directory

Getting ready to party

Directory

333
333 OLD STREET EC1
TEL: 0171 739 5949
⊖ Old Street.

Annex
1a Dean Street W1
Tel: 0171 287 9608
⊖ Tottenham Ct Rd.

Aquarium
255 Old Street EC1
Tel: 0171-251 6136
⊖ Old Street

The Arches
53 Southwark Street SE1
Tel: 0171 207 2980
⊖ London Bridge

Bagley's Studios
York Way N1
Tel: 0171 278 2777
⊖ King's Cross.

Bar Cuba
11 Kensington High St W8
Tel: 0171 938 4137
⊖ High St. Kensington

Bar Rumba
36 Shaftesbury Avenue W1
Tel: 0171 287 2715
⊖ Piccadilly.

Bar Tiempo
Pentonville Road N1
Tel: 0171 837 5387
⊖ Angel.

Blue Angel
Torrens Street City Road EC1
Tel: 0171 837 9421
⊖ Angel.

The Borderline
5 Manette Street W1
Tel: 0171 734 2095
⊖ Tottenham Court Rd.

The Bunker Bar
Bagley's Studios
York Way N1
Tel: 0171 278 2777
⊖ King's Cross.

Camden Palace
Camden High St NW1
Tel: 0171 387 0428
⊖ Camden Town.

Chocolate Bar
57 Berkeley Square W1
Tel: 0171 499 7850
⊖ Green Park.

The Chunnel Club
101 Tinworth Street
Albert Embankment SE1
Tel: 0171 820 1702
⊖ Vauxhall.

The Clinic
13 Gerrard Street W1
Tel: 0171 734 9836
⊖ Leicester Square

Club Extreme 15 Ganton
Street W1 Tel: 0171 494
1115). ⊖ Oxford Circus.

The Colosseum
1 Nine Elms Lane SW8
Tel: 0171-720 3609
⊖ Vauxhall.

The Complex 1 Parkfield
Street N1
Tel: 0171 288 1986
⊖ Angel.

Corks 28 Binney Street W1
Tel: 0171 408 0100
⊖ Bond Street.

The Cross
Goods Way Depot
York Way N1
Tel: 0171 837 0828
⊖ King's Cross.

The Crossbar
257 Pentonville Road N1
Tel: 0171 837 3218
⊖ King's Cross.

Cuba Bar
11 Kensington High St W8
Tel: 0171 483 2393
⊖ Finchley Road.

The Dogstar
389 Coldharbour Lane SW9
Tel: 0171-733 7515
⊖ Brixton.

The Dragon
Tooley Street SE1
Tel:0171 403 4445
⊖ London Bridge

Electric Ballroom
Camden High St NW1
Tel: 0171 485 9006
⊖ Camden Town

Equinox
Leicester Square WC2
Tel: 0171 437 1446
⊖ Leicester Square.

The Forum
Highgate Road, NW5
Tel: 0171 344 0044
⊖ /BR: Kentish Town.

Directory

The Fridge
Town Hall Parade SW2
Tel: 0171 326 5100
⊖/BR: Brixton.

The Gardening Club
The Piazza WC2
Tel: 0171 497 3153
⊖ Covent Garden.

The Gass Club
Whitcomb Street WC2
Tel: 0171 839 3922
⊖ Piccadilly.

Global Cafe
13 Golden Square Wl
Tel: 0171 287 2242
⊖ Piccadilly.

Gossips
69 Dean Street W1
Tel: 0171 434 4480
⊖ Leicester Square

Hanover Grand
17 Hanover Street Wl
Tel: 0171 499 7977
⊖ Oxford Circus.

HQ
West Yard NW1
Tel: 0171 485 6044
⊖ Camden Town.

The Imperial Gardens
299 Camberwell New Rd SE5
Tel: 0171 252 6000
⊖ Oval.

Insomnia
11 Wardour Street Wl
Tel: 0171 287 1220
⊖ Leicester Square.

The Islington Bar
342 Caledonian Road Nl
Tel: 0171 609 4917
⊖ King's Cross.

Jazz Cafe
5 Parkway NW1
Tel: 0171 916 6060
⊖ Camden Town.

K-Bar
266a Fulham Road SW10
Tel: 0171 352 6200
⊖/Fulham Broadway

LA 2
157 Charing Cross Rd
WC2
Tel: 0171 434 0403
⊖ Tottenham Ct. Rd.

Legends
29 Old Burlington St W1
Tel: 0171 437 9933
⊖ Piccadilly.

Leisure Lounge
121 Holborn EC1
Tel: 0171 242 1345
⊖ Chancery Lane.

The crowded dancefloor of the Hippodrome in Leicester Square

Directory

Le Scandale
53 Berwick Street W1
Tel: 0171437 6830
⊖ Oxford Circus.

Loughborough Hotel
Loughborough Road SW9
Tel: 0171 771 3134
⊖ /BR: Brixton.

Macadam Building
Surrey Street, WC2
Tel: 0171 836 7132
⊖ Temple.

Madame Jo Jo's
Brewer Street W1
Tel: 0171 734 2473
⊖ Piccadilly.

Medicine Bar
181 Upper Street N1
Tel: 0171 704 8056
⊖ Highbury & Islington.

Ministry Of Sound
103 Gaunt Street SE1
Tel: 0171 378 6528
⊖ Elephant & Castle.

Ormonds
91 Jermyn Street SW1
Tel: 0171 930 2842
⊖ Piccadilly.

Oxygen
18 Irving Street W1
Tel: 0171 930 0905
⊖ Leicester Square

The Plug
Stockwell Road SW9
Tel: 0171 274 3879
⊖ Stockwell.

Po Na Na
Upper Street N1
Tel: 0171 359 6191
⊖ Highbury & Islington

Po Na Na
20 Kensington Church St
Tel: 0171 795 6656
⊖ Kensington High St.

The Powerhaus
Seven Sisters Road N4
Tel: 0171 344 0044
⊖ /BR: Finsbury Park.

Rock Garden
Covent Garden WC2
Tel: 0171 240 3961
⊖ Covent Garden.

Ronnie Scott's
Frith Street Wl
Tel: 0171 439 0747
⊖ Leicester Square.

Smithfield's
341 Farringdon Street EC1
Tel: 0171 236 4266
⊖ Farringdon.

Sound Republic
10 Wardour Street W1
Tel: 0171 287 1010
⊖ Oxford Circus.

The Spot
29 Maiden Lane WC2
Tel: 0171 379 5900
⊖ Charing Cross

Subterania
Acklam Road W10
Tel: 0181 960 4590
⊖ Ladbroke Grove.

SW1
191 Victoria Street SW1
Tel:0171 630 8980
⊖ Victoria.

Tactical Bar
27 D'Arblay Street W1
Tel: 0171 287 2823
⊖ Oxford Circus.

Turnmills
63b Clerkenwell Road EC1
Tel: 0171 250 3409
⊖ Farringdon.

The Underworld
174 Camden High St NW1
Tel: 0171 482 1932
⊖ Camden Town.

The Velvet Room
143 Charing Cross Rd WC2
Tel: 0171 439 4655
⊖ Tottenham Ct Rd.

Vibe Bar
91 Brick Lane E1
Tel: 0171 247 1231
⊖ Highbury & Islington.

The Wag
Wardour Street Wl
Tel:01 71 437 5534
⊖ Piccadilly Circus.

Zazoom Bar
New Burlington St Wl
Tel: 0171 287 1991
⊖ Oxford Circus.

WKD
18 Kentish Town Road
Tel: 0171 795 6656
⊖ Camden Town

Hotels
Where To Stay

Before making your hotel reservation you should establish what you want from your accommodation. Decide what is important to you - location, size and amenities. Then find out what is available within your price range.

Ask your travel agent for an up-to-date list of hotels. If they haven't got one, try the tourist office for the country in which you wish to travel.

Most guides grade hotels and other accommodation in categories from luxurious to cheap. Luxurious hotels should provide you with everything from a remote control television in your room to breakfast in bed in the morning. In cheap hotels you may find your bathroom is at the end of the corridor and the sheets are not starched.

If you decide on a large 'chain hotel' you will always know what to expect whether you are in Delhi, Dallas or Dublin. In fact you may not even notice the difference. But most hotels have a personality of their own which may be hard to discern beforehand over the phone. Always confirm all bookings by letter or fax to avoid any confusion that may arise.

London hotels usually charge by the person rather than by the room and in the 'chain' hotels may include a Continental or English breakfast.

Check whether value added tax and service is included in the price and if you are pleased with the service a small 'tip' to the chambermaid is usually much appreciated.

Most of the larger hotels have some fine restaurants and some serve afternoon tea. Travelling businessmen will find they have conference facilities, secretarial services and all the latest communication equipment at their disposal. Booking well in advance is absolutely essential. Not only does it guarantee a firm booking it gives you greater choice.

In the following pages we have given you the choice of small and friendly country house hotels. Where prices are indicated, they are approximate as special terms can be negotiated depending on the time of year. Some have special offers, or weekend breaks that include theatre tickets to a top West End Show or some other form of entertainment. Ask before confirming your reservation.

Please note: For up to date prices please check with the hotel of your selection before confirming your reservation.

Thomas Cook

Hotel Reservations Rail Station
Buckingham Palace Rd Victoria SW1
Tel: 0171 233 6751
Open daily from 8am-11pm
Offer you the choice of a five star hotel, bed and breakfast or a hostel

Hotel Finders

20 Bell Lane Hendon NW4
Tel: 0181 202 7000/0988
Open Mon-Fri 9am-5.30pm
Sat from 9am- 1pm
Have a wide range of services, including free hotel and conference booking facilities.

Hot Line Reservations

134 Lexham Gardens Kensington W8
Tel: 0171 373 9531 (24 hour service)
Have existing contracts with a large number of hotels and operate this service free to the hotel guest.

BHRC

10 Buckingham Palace Road SW1
Freephone 0800 28 28 28
A hotel booking service for all classes of accommodation for business people, tourists, students, individuals and groups

Group Bookings

For group bookings and theatre tickets please telephone our hot line:
Telephone: 0171 402 1946
Facsimile: 0171 402 4161
E mail: declare@netdirect.co.uk

Basil Street Hotel

8 Basil Street Knightsbridge SW3
Tel: 0171 581 3311
Total rooms: 92

Cost: Single £125 Double £185
Advance booking: 2 weeks
Within a parcel wrap of Harrods, this was a very popular hotel when ladies came to London to do their shopping in Knightsbridge and still manages to retain its charm and high quality service.

Beaufort

33 Beaufort Gardens SW3
Tel: 0171 584 5252
Total rooms: 28

Cost: Single £170 Double £200
Advance booking: 2 weeks
Continental breakfast, free champagne by the glass and afternoon teas are on offer when you stay at this delightful little hotel that is situated quite close to Harrods and Harvey Nichols. Price also includes membership of a health club and airport or station transfers.

Blakes

33-35 Roland Gardens
South Kensington SW7
Tel: 0171 370 6701
Total rooms: 52

Cost: Single £155 Double £220
Advance booking: 2 weeks
A very stylish hotel is one of the first in what is now known as Town House Hotels. Each one of the 52 bedrooms has been individually designed by the owner, the former actress Anouska Hempel. This is the ideal place to stay if you want to avoid the hustle and bustle of some of the larger hotels in the West End.

Brown's

24-24 Dover Street W1
Tel: 0171 493 6020
Total rooms:116
Cost: Single £250 Double: £280
Advance booking: 4 weeks
The original Mr Brown was butler to
Lord Byron and the hotel he founded
became home from home for the
gentry. It still retains its charm and
character despite being owned by one
of the larger groups.

Capital

Basil Street SW3
Tel: 0171 589 5171
Total rooms: 48
Cost: Single: £180 Double: £235
Advance booking: 4 weeks
This sophisticated, yet informal hotel
is just behind Knightsbridge Tube
Station and has an excellent Michelin
starred restaurant and a wine bar

Portobello

22 Stanley Gardens W11
Tel: 0171 727 2777
Total rooms: 25 Cost: Single: £115
Double: £155 inclusive.

Continental .Breakfast Advance
booking: 2 weeks
Extremely popular with celebs from
the music industry and with the
added bonus of a 24 hour food and
drinks license. Guests also qualify for
a 20% discount if dining at Julie's
Restaurant and Wine Bar and free
admission and use of facilities at the
Lambton Place Health Club. Both are
within ten minutes walk of the hotel.

Halcyon

81 Holland Park W11
Tel: 0171 727 7288
Total rooms: 43
Cost: Single £165 Double £270
Advance booking: 3 weeks
This fashionable hotel is situated
near Holland Park and far from the
madding crowds of London's West
End. They have a really excellent
restaurant known as 'The Room at
the Halcyon' which opens on to a
small garden. Catrina Hall's very
tasteful interior design is both
luxurious and soothing. A very
reliable around the clock room
service is also at hand.

Wonderful views can be enjoyed whilst staying at The Conrad Hilton in Chelsea Harbour

The delightful dining room in the Halcyon Hotel

★ Five Star Hotels

BERKELEY HOTEL Wilton Place SW1	Tel: 0171 235 6000
CHURCHILL 30 Portman Square W1	Tel: 0171 486 5800
CLARIDGE'S Brook Street W1	Tel: 0171 629 8860
CONNAUGHT 16 Carlos Place W1	Tel: 0171 499 7070
THE DORCHESTER Park Lane W1	Tel: 0171 629 8888
THE LANDMARK 222 Marylebone Road NW1	Tel: 0171 631 8000
THE LANESBOROUGH Hyde Park Corner SW1	Tel: 0171 259 5599
LONDON MARRIOTT HOTEL Grosvenor Square W1	Tel: 0171 493 1232
MAYFAIR INTERCONTINENTAL HOTEL Stratton Street W1	Tel: 0171 629 7777
THE MERIDIEN 21 Piccadilly W1	Tel: 0171 734 8000
RITZ HOTEL Piccadilly W1	Tel: 0171 493 8181
SAVOY The Strand WC2	Tel: 0171 836 4343
SHERATON PARK TOWER 101 Knightsbridge SW1	Tel: 0171 235 8050
WALDORF Aldwych WC2	Tel: 0171 836 2400

★ Four Star Hotels

CHESTERFIELD MAYFAIR HOTEL 35 Charles Street W1..........Tel: 0171 491 2622
THE LONDON METROPOLE 225 Edgware Road W2 ....Tel: 0171 402 4141
KENSINGTON PALACE THISTLE De Vere Gardens W8 ....Tel: 0171 937 8121
MARLBOROUGH CREST Bloomsbury Street WC1 ....Tel: 0171 636 5601
MONTCALM Great Cumberland Place W1 ....Tel: 0171 402 4288
MOUNTBATTEN PLAZA HOTEL 20 Monmouth Street WC2......Tel: 0171 836 4300
PARK LANE HOTEL Park Lane W1 ....Tel: 0171 499 6321
THE PORTMAN 22 Portman Square ....Tel: 0171 486 5844
ROYAL LANCASTER Lancaster Gate W2 ....Tel: 0171 262 6737
RUSSELL HOTEL Russell Square WC1 ....Tel: 0171 837 6470
SWALLOW INTERNATIONAL HOTEL 147 Cromwell Rd SW5 ...Tel: 0171 370 4200
WASHINGTON HOTEL 5 Curzon Street W1 ....Tel: 0171 499 7000
WAVERLEY HOUSE HOTEL 130-134 Southampton Row WC1 Tel: 0171 833 3691
WESTBURY Conduit Street W1 ....Tel: 0171 629 7755
WHITE HOUSE The Albany Street NW1...................................Tel: 0171 387 1200
WHITES 90-92 Lancaster Gate W2...Tel: 0171 262 2711
CHARLES DICKENS Lancaster Gate W2 ....Tel: 0171 262 5090

★ Three Star Hotels

CLIVE HOTEL at Hampstead Primrose Hill Road NW3 ......Tel: 0171 586 2233
IMPERIAL Russell Square WC2...Tel: 0171 278 7871
LA PLACE 17 Nottingham Place Near Baker Street W1..........Tel: 0171 486 2323
MANDEVILLE HOTEL 8-12 Mandeville Place W1 ....Tel: 0171 935 5599
MOSTYN 4 Bryanston Street Near Baker Street W1 ....Tel: 0171 935 2361
MOUNT ROYAL HOTEL Bryanston Street Marble Arch W1......Tel: 0171 629 8040
THE PARK COURT 75 Lancaster Gate W2...............................Tel: 0171 402 4272
THE PLAZA ON HYDE PARK Lancaster Gate W2 ....Tel: 0171 262 5022
RUBENS HOTEL Buckingham Palace Road ....Tel: 0171 834 6600
ST. ERMIN'S Caxton Street SW1 ....Tel: 0171 222 7888
STRAND PALACE 372 The Strand WC2 ....Tel: 0171 836 8080
TAVISTOCK Tavistock Square WC1 ....Tel: 0171 636 8383

Dating Agencies

Dateline
23 Abingdon Road Kensington W8
Tel: 0171 938 1011
Probably the most famous, and with an enormous 40,000 membership. There is bound to be someone right up your street possibly literally. It costs £150 for the standard service, which is assessment by questionnaire only, with no interview, or £450 for the Gold Service in which you chat to a Dateline representative, adding a human element to what is essentially matchmaking by computer. For both services you get a minimum of five dates. Dateline prefers people to have sufficient command of 'English' to write a letter or converse fluently. The recently bereaved and divorced are asked to cool off for a while before entering the dating game.

Drawing Down the Moon
165 Kensington High Street W8
Tel: 0171 937 6263
The name of this agency is taken from a Greek myth, and the clientele sought after are the intelligentsia: people who know their gluteus maximus from their humerus. Flicking through their files, I noticed that a great many of the candidates on DDM's files read novels, so a knowledge of recent bestsellers may come in handy. Mary Balfour says that her worst disaster running the agency was when she matched up two people who were recently divorced. However the divorcees were kind enough to say that Mary had done a good job in bringing them together as they did have more in common than anyone else on their books. The cost is approximately £650 with a £100 discount for joining at the first meeting. DDM has about 800 people on its books, and deals with an age range of 25-45.

The Picture Dating Agency
29 Villiers Street WC2
Tel: 0171 839 8884
Offers two services, both similar to those of Dateline but about half the price: £65 for an assessment by questionnaire without an interview, and £140 for which you get interviewed. Seeing the photograph of your prospective date is of the utmost importance at this agency, so people who are no oil paintings so to speak, but have great personalities are advised to go to an agency where pictures are not used for selection.

Hedi Fisher
110 Gloucester Avenue NW1
Tel: 0171 722 0744
Susanne Sander doesn't believe in showing clients photos of potential lovers; because the photo could remind you of your horrible neighbour or old headmaster. Here you get a minimum of six introductions a year, and they do the selecting. Numbers of members are in the hundreds but not thousands, and apparently also have a number of Russian and Oriental women on their books looking for relationships. The cost is £250 for a minimum of six introductions a year.

Karen Mooney -The Matchmaker

If you enter into a relationship with someone , you are put 'on hold' meaning that if the relationship doesn't work out you can select new dates until you have reached your quota.

Sara Eden Introductions

38 Thames Street Windsor Berkshire
Tel: 01753830350
Billed as the introduction agency for beautiful people with about 2,000 people on their books, mainly graduates and high flyers. The cost here is £430 plus vat, with a reduction if you sign up on the the first meeting. If you enter into a relationship with someone, you are put 'on hold' meaning that if the relationship doesn't work out you can select new dates until you have reached your quota.

The English Connection

20 Albion Street Broadstairs Kent
Tel: 01843 863 322

The English Connection puts English men together with American women and has a sister company, English Rose, that does it vice versa. All you have to do is fill in a questionnaire and you are initially matched with five likely prospects. It is circulated with your photograph and you get to hear from anyone interested. The annual fee - is: £345 for English Connection, £499 for English Rose. The agency has been established for over years and boasts very high success rate during that time.

Only Lunch

Suite 116 64/78 Kingsway WC2
Tel: 0171 404 8691
Freephone: 0800 908900
Established in June 1997
The cost is £636 plus vat per year. This is based on the American idea that you split the bill on the first meeting. You are allowed 10 dates in the course of a year and if you should strike lucky before exhausting your quota you are put on 'hold'.

Significant Others

14 South Molton Street W1
Tel 0171 499 5939
This is a bureau for professional gay men charging an annual fee of £450 and as many introductions as it takes to form a long term relationship withi that period

Watercolours

11-12 Hanover Square W1
Tel: 0171 629 3185
Age range 25/55; Approx.: 700 Clients
The concept of a singles gallery is an American import. Each client provides a large photo and a comprehensive portfolio of their character, preferences and previous relationship history. These are then exhibited, so to speak, in the gallery. The cost is £790 for two years and there is no limit to the number of dates you can have in that time. Various services are offered.

Internet Cafes

Wannabe a surfer and get hooked on the net? Internet Cafes are the place to be for computer nerds - you can play games, watch clips from movies even check your email: The following cafes offer snacks, computers that are already hooked up to the Internet, as well as training. Don't be scared to surf while you sip.

Buzz Bar
97 Portobello Road W11
Tel: 0171 460 4906
http//www.enterprise.net/england
More an internet pub, rather than a cafe, very relaxing with pale green decor and machinery with attachments to hold drinks and ashtrays. You can enjoy champagne and oysters while you surf the net.

Cafe Internet
22-24 Buckingham Palace Road
Victoria SW1
Tel: 0171 233 5786
http://www.cafeinternet.co.uk
If you are new to the net this is the place for you. A crash course is available at £10 for half - an - hour. A two hour introduction with tool information costs £25 and a one-day intensive session costs £250. They will take groups in their training room, but advance booking is necessary.

Cyberia
Piccadilly Circus W1
Tel: 0171 287 2242
The original London internet cafe, Open Mon-Fri 8am-11.30pm;Sat 10am- 11.30pm; Sun 1pm-11pm
This laid-back but busy cafe opened three years ago. There are fourteen terminals and three Sega Saturn game stations.

Cyberia
39 Whitfield Street W1
Tel:0171 209 0983
http://channel.cyberiacafe.net
This was the first internet cafe, established in 1994 and now with branches in Ealing and Kingston upon Thames. Very popular with visitors checking their email and sending email postcards to the folks back home. Concessionary rates of £1.90 per half hour for students. Loud and laid back.

Global Cafe
15 Golden Square W1
Tel: 0171 287 2242
http.//www.cyberspy.net
Cafe society and computer technology
come together in this spacious art
cafe, proving the versatility of the
internet web. Seven PC's computers
are available and charged at £2.75 per
half hour.

The Spider Café
195 Portobello Road W11
Tel : 0171 229 2990
http://www.spidercafe.co.uk.
The place for parties - kids or
corporate entertainment. Even film
Netheads use the equipment here to
keep in touch with Hollywood. Staff
are available to help beginners and
ensure that surfers have fun.

InternetCafe
Queensway Shopping Arcade
23/25 Queensway W2
Telephone: 0171 313 9933
Open Mon-Sun from 10am-10pm
Access to all internet services at £6
per hour or 10pence a minute.Happy
hour is between 10am-1pm at £5 per
hour. Coffee, tea and soft drinks are
served free of charge to all users.

Backspace
Clink Street SEI
Tel: 0171 234 0804

Hands On
Old Brompton Road SW7
Tel: 0171 581 3399

Interc@fe
Great Portland Street WI
Tel: 0171 631 0063

Network City
Marylebone High Street WI
Tel: 0171 224 4400

The Vibe Bar
Brick Lane E1
Tel: 0171 247 3479

Dillons Cyber St@tion
Gower Street WC l
Tel: 0171 636 1577

Input-Output
Marylebone Library NWI
Tel: 0171 486 3161

Getting Away - Airlines

AEROFLOT Russian International Airlines 70 Piccadilly W1 ..Tel: 0171 355 2233

AIR AFRIQUE 4th Floor 86 Hatton Garden EC1 ....Tel: 0171 430 0284

AIR ALGERIE 10 Baker Street W1 ....Tel: 0171 487 5903

AIR CHINA 41 Grosvenor Gardens SW1 ....Tel: 0171 630 7678

AIR FRANCE Colet House Hammersmith Road W6 ....Tel: 08450 845111

AIR LINGUS 83 Staines Road Hounslow Middlesex ....Tel: 0181 899 4747

AIR MAURITIUS 49 Conduit Street W1 ....Tel: 0171 434 4375

AIR UK London Stanstead Airport Essex ....Tel: 01293 535353

ALITALIA 27 Piccadilly W1 .... Tel: 0171 602 7111

AMERICAN AIRLINES 15 Berkeley Street W1 ....Tel: 0345 789 789

AUSTRIAN AIRLINES 10 Wardour Street W1 ....Tel: 0171 434 7350

BRITISH AIRWAYS LBTC 200 Buckingham Palace Rd SW1 ...Tel: 09904 44000

DELTA AIRLINES Oakfield Court Consort Way Horley Surrey .Tel: 0800 414767

GULF AIR 10 Albermarle Street W1 ....Tel: 0171 408 1717

IBERIA AIRLINES OF SPAIN 11-12 Haymarket SW1 ....Tel: 0171 830 0011

JAPAN AIRLINES Hanover Court 5 Hanover Square W1 ....Tel: 0345 747700

KLM ROYAL DUTCH AIRLINES ....Tel: 0990 074074

KUWAIT AIRWAYS 16 Baker Street W1..................................Tel: 0171 412 0006

LUFTHANSA 7 Conduit Street W1 ....Tel: 0345 737747

MALAYSIA AIRLINES 61 Piccadilly W1 ....Tel: 0171 341 2000

OLYMPIC AIRLINES 11 Conduit Street W1 ....Tel: 0171 409 2400

RYANAIR LINES Enterprise House Stansted Airport Essex ......Tel: 0541 569 569

QUANTAS AIRLINES 182 Strand WC2 ....Tel: 0345 737767

SAS SCANDINAVIAN AIRWAYS 52 Conduit Street W1 ....Tel: 0171 465 0123

SWISSAIR Swiss Centre Wardour Street W1 ....Tel: 0171 434 7300

TAP AIR PORTUGAL Gillingham Street SW1 ....Tel: 0171 828 2092

THAI AIRLINES 41 Albermarle Street W1 ....Tel: 0171 499 9113

UNITED AIRLINES 193 Piccadilly W1 ....Tel: 08458 444777

Greyhound Racing

It all began back in 1926 when we had mass unemployment and were in deep, deep recession and now greyhound racing is being rediscovered by a new young generation as thousands flock to the dozens of newly modernised luxury stadia throughout the country - it's the second most popular audience participation sport in the land, second only to football.

Forget the cloth cap image, the tired old jokes about going to the dogs, get in with the 'in crowd' and hare down to your local Stadium for the night of your life. London is surrounded by greyhound racing tracks; Wembley, Wimbledon and Walthamstow, Hackney, Catford. Crayford and Coral Romford. The racing starts at around 7.30pm with entrance fees around £3 - £5 and all have parking facilities.

As you arrive the thing that impresses you most is the sheer size of these venues which can cater for up to 10,000 people. The excitement generated is infectious as the girls parade the six hounds competing in their colourful numbered jackets.

If one of the dog stops to have a 'pee' it's supposed to be a good omen because it will be racing that much lighter, and the odds which are flashed up on computer operated screens are liable to 'shorten'.

Going to the dogs: A great way to spend an evening.

You will be pampered by discreet waitresses and lovely ladies who will place your bets for you and if you should be so lucky, they will also collect your winnings. Should you be in the dark about betting - and its finer points, you will not be short of helpful advice.

If horse racing was the sport of kings, greyhound racing was the sport of paupers. Hence the cloth-cap image that has so bedevilled the sport's reputation until now. There is a theory that first time gamblers always win so, however bizzare your choice, you may well find many new friends only too willing to help and probably follow your lead.

Stadiums

Catford Greyhound Stadium
Adenmore Rd Catford Bridge SE6
Tel: 0181 690 8000
135 seat restaurant
Saturday: A la carte only.
Racing Mon, Thu and Sats at 7.30pm.

Coral Romford Stadium
London Road Romford Essex
Tel: 01707 762345
240 seat restaurant.
Racing Mon, Wed, Fri and Sat 7.30pm
(Selected Thursday .afternoons
from 1pm)
For a weekend or mid-week jaunt
Coral also race at their Brighton
Stadium.

Ladbroke Crayford Stadium
Stadium Way Crayford Kent
Tel: 01322 557836
Large restaurant with two 2 bars.
Tables for six. T.V. monitors, luxury seating and top class food. Full range of beers and spirits and superb wine list. Fully air conditioned. Unlimited parking. Racing Monday, Thursday and Saturdays. First race at 7.30pm Saturdays also 11.07am (on Thursday times may vary).

Wembley Stadium
Empire Way Middlesex
Tel: 0181 902 8833
Restaurant 220 seats.
Racing Mon, Wed and Fri at 7.30pm
Well stocked bars.

Wimbledon Stadium
Plough Lane Wimbledon SW17
Tel: 0181 946 8000
Racing: Tue, Fri and Sats at 7.30pm.
A large luxurious restaurant and first class food, licensed bars. Full ranges of beers, spirits and wine list second to none. T.V. monitors, great service and fully air conditioned with unlimited parking.

Walthamstow Stadium
Chingford Road E4
General enquiries Tel: 0181 531 4255
Restaurant: 0181 527 7277.
Racing Tue and Thu 7.30pm-10.15pm;
Sat 7.30pm-10.30pm
U:Walthamstow Central/Victoria Line
One of the longest established racing stadiums in London. Corporate boxes and excellent dining facilities.

Gay

What is it that makes London the cutting edge of the world's gay clubland? Is it the very diversity, the cosmopolitan concentration of night hawks that forms the scene? Is it the ever-growing, ever-changing array of one-nighters run by discerning young entrepreneurs and DJs with a bag of new tricks? Indeed, new establishments throw their doors open all the time. Long-toothed promoters are forever bent on experimenting with new ideas and formulae, thus stretching the pink pound further and further.

After all, gays are notorious for having a disposable income and the market is booming to the point that more businesses want their share of the cake.

Virgin stores organize regular gay-shoppers events, British Airways have set package holidays for gay travellers, the list goes on...

Major yearly events like Freedom Fair, Summer Rites and Pride (which, being the largest annual one-day free

Brazilian Go Go dancer Joao strutting his stuff at the Fridge in Brixton

festival in Europe, attracts an audience of around 200,000) and are a direct reflection of the boom.

It seems like in the late 1990s, people want to leave behind their inhibitions and the repression to live their life, be themselves. That's the beauty of being in London, as there'll always be somewhere to go to satisfy the most fastidious.

Gay clubs have a reputation for being more fun and outrageous than their straight counterparts and that's because they are. The easing of the licensing laws in the '90s has meant that clubbers can drink and dance around the clock in many places (Trade, Heaven, The Fridge etc.), if that's what they want to do. It is good to have a choice.

The scene also caters for radically different sections of the community, so you can afford to be selective. The fact that you might want to patronise one niterie rather than another always proves to be a personal thing. Many factors come into the equation like location, space, decor, clientele, door and drink prices. But, first and foremost the music policy wins hands down.

Promoters know that the more name DJs they splash over their flyers, the happier their bank managers are likely to be. Bear in mind the other side of the coin as

well: having a star behind the wheels of steel doesn't always guarantee a good time. Often 'no' name DJs will not only save you a packet, but show you a better time on the dancefloor.

Punters soon find that out and know how to patronise a club that can deliver the music they want to hear, rather than follow celebrities for the sake of it. It is always a good idea to check out what's on the playlist before you commit yourself.

Whether your musical tastes lie in garage house, handbag, techno, drum n' bass, britpop, nu-soul, hip hop, funk, jazz, ambient or easy, you'll find that there'll always be a place they are catered for. Remember, whatever you're into, be it the incongruous, the frankly grotesque or the plain casual, there'll be a knees-up for you. Read on and get out there. Happy clubbing!

Gay Bars

Benjys
562a Mile End Road, E3
Tel: 0181 980 6427
U: Mile End
Sun: Disco 9pm-1am.Resident D.J.
This has been a popular Sunday night
for some years now, attracting a good
East End crowd. Next door to Mile
End station.

The Black Cap
170 Camden High Street NW1

Tel: 0171 428 2721
Mon-Sat 9pm-2am

A bustling and unsophisticated crowd
dance to Seventies and Eighties pop
in laid-back Camden Town

They said smart but casual.

Bromptons
294 Old Brompton Road SW5
Tel: 0171 370 1344
Mon-Sat 6pm-2am Sun 5-12midnight
(Nearest U: Earls Court
Changeable Cabaret every Mon & Thu
and Tuesday is leather night
Dated surroundings but very popular
with a mainly cloney crowd.

Central Station
37 Wharfedale Rd Kings Cross N1
Tel: 0171 278 3294
Nearest U: Kings Cross
Mon -Wed 5pm 2am; Thu 5pm -3am;
Friday 5pm -4am; Sat 12noon-4am;
Sun 12noon -midnight
Popular modern bar with a regular
programme of strippers, cabaret acts,
'theme' nights and basement club
'Underground'.

Comptons
53 Old Compton Street, W1
Tel: 0171 437 4445
Nearest U: Piccadilly Circus
Mon-Sat 12-11pm Sun 7-10.30
Traditional, unpretentious and very
loud pub which, despite the trend for
shiny new café/bars. Busy, but seems
to go in and out of fashion.

The Edge
11 Soho Square
Tel: 0171 439 1313
Mon-Sat 12noon-1am and Sun
12noon 10.30pm
Nearest U: Tottenham Court Road
Stylish café/bar. Very mixed (straight
/gay), especially daytime and after
work, but we like the fab designer
surroundings.

Gay Bars

The Bar Shoreditch/
Chariots Cafe Bar
Chariots House Fairchild Street
Near Liverpool Street EC2
Tel: 0171 247 5222
Nearest U: Liverpool Street
Mon-Sat 11am-11pm; Sun 12-10.30pm
A spacious and friendly cafe/bar
situated between Old Street and
Liverpool Street. DJ's and cabaret
nightly. Adequate bar snacks and
alert service.

The Box
Seven Dials
32-34 Monmouth Street WC2
Tel: 0171 240 5828
Nearest U: Leicester Square
Drinks, food and coffee are served
daily in this modern bar to a very
mixed Covent Garden crowd.

King William IV
75 Hampstead High Street NW3
Tel: 0171 435 5747
Mon-Sat 12noon -11pm Sun 12noon-
10.30pm
Very well-known traditional and
popular North London pub boasting
an extensive garden. Comfortable,
friendly and mostly male.

Kudos
10 Adelaide Street WC2
Tel: 0171 379 4573
Mon-Sat 10am-11pm;
Sun 12noon- 10.30pm
Modern ground floor café/bar, with a
good value no-frills menu, and a
darker and more cruisy basement bar
(Arena).

Julia and her promoter friend at The Candy
Club a popular lesbian venue in
Carlisle Street W1 -

Vauxhall Tavern
327 Kennington Lane SE11
Tel: 0171 582 0833
Nearest U: Vauxhall
The original and now almost an
institution for drag acts. Sunday is
club night with DJ.

Village Soho
81 Wardour Street Piccadilly W1
Nearest U: Oxford Street or Piccadilly
Mon-Sat noon-11 Sun 7.30-10.30
Very busy bar on 3 levels with cafe,
disco area. Predominantly male
orientated. Food is served up to 5pm.
Gets much livelier and more clubby
as the evening progresses.

Whilst every care has been taken to
obtain accurate and reliable information, it is advisable to telephone the
venue before setting out.

Substation
Falconberg Court
off Charing Cross Road W1
Tel: 0171 287 9608
Nearest U: Tottenham Court Road
Mon-Thur 9pm-3am Fri 9pm-4am
Industrial-style décor with wire
fencing sets the tone for this small
cruise bar/club.

The Yard
57 Rupert Street Piccadilly W1
Tel: 0171 437 2653
Open Mon-Sat: 12noon-11pm ;
Sun 12noon--10.30pm
Nearest U: Piccadilly Circus
Two fashionable and stylish bars:
Enclosed outdoor courtyard, and loft
bar with balcony and outdoor
staircase. Relaxed laid-back
atmosphere and fortune tellers who
will tell you what's in store for you.

BJ's White Swan
556 Commercial Road E14
Tel: 0171 780 9870
Mon 9pm-1am; Tue-Thu 9pm-2am
Fri/Sat 9-pm 2am
Nearest U: Aldgate East
Busy and unpretentious East London
pub with drag acts and strippers
performing nightly.

Gay Clubs

Club Industria
9 Hanover Street W1
Tel: 0171 493 0689
Nearest U: Oxford Circus
A lesbian and gay dance night
is held here at least one night a week
between 10.30pm-4am. Also mixed
gay night with 'infectious rhythms
and uplifting vocals'.

Girls just wanna have fun

Gay Clubs

FF Club
Turnmills
63b Clerkenwell Road EC2
Tel: 0171 250 3409
Sun only 7pm-5am
Nearest U: Farringdon
House and techno for a stylish,
hedonistic crowd that know how to
party with a capital P.

Fruit Machine
Heaven, Villiers Street WC2
Under The Arches Charing Cross
Tel: 0171 930 2020
Wed only 10.30pm- 3am
Busy midweek club. Powder Room
(drag bar) and disco kitchen.

G.A.Y. Good As You
At LA, 1 and 2, The Astoria
157 Charing Cross Road WC2
Tel: 0171 434 9592
Nearest U: Tottenham Court Road
A major club night, bringing some
choice back to Fridays! PA's have
already included top acts.

Heaven
The Arches Villiers Street WC2
Tel: 0171 930 2020
Mon-Fri 10.30pm -3am Sat 10.30pm-
6am; Sun 3pm-midnight
Nearest U: Charing Cross
UK's largest gay club that recently
underwent major refurbishment.
Enormous dancefloors, bars, games
and shops. Saturday night Sunday
morning appears to be more popular
than ever.

The three wise men enjoying themselves at the re-launch of **Heaven**

Limelight

136 Shaftesbury Avenue
Cambridge Circus W1
Tel: 0171 434 0572
U: Tottenham Court Road
Sunday night is gay-night between
6pm-11pm in this great club venue,
housed inside an old church.

Love Muscle

The Fridge (Sat only 10pm - 6am
Town Hall Parade Brixton SW2
Tel: 0171 326 5100
Nearest U: Brixton
Despite the very commercial dance
music this huge dark venue is lively,
friendly, and always packed. Still one
of the best gay clubs in London.

Trade at Turnmills

63b Clerkenwell Road.EC2
Tel 0171 250 3409
Sun only 10pm -8am
Nearest U: Farringdon
Original and pioneering all-nighter.
Not always as busy as it used to be,
but still providing hardcore house for
those who want to party all night long.

Wayout Club

9pm-3am Weekly at Tiffany's
28 Minories EC3
Tel:0181 363 0948
(For up-to-date information)
Nearest U:Aldgate/Tower Hill
Berlinesque club and bar for a
wonderfully diverse mix of gays,
straights, trannies, drag queens and
theatrical friends.

Dressing down.

Candy Bar

4 Carlisle Street
off Soho Square W1
Tel: 0171 494 4041
Nearest U:Tottenham Court Road
Open: Mon-Fri 5pm-11pm; Sat 11am-
11pm; Sun 5pm-10.30 Lesbian bar
A relatively new Lesbian Bar in the
hub of Soho.The club is on three
floors and they claim to be the
biggest in the UK. Lap dancing on
Wednesday night. Men are welcome
as guests .

Drill Hall Women Only Bar

16 Chenies Street WC1
Tel: 0171 631 1353
Mondays 6pm-11pm.
Nearest U: Holborn
Popular weekly women's bar with
soft music and great prices.

Gay Saunas

Pleasuredrome Central
125 Alaska Street SE1
Tel: 0171 633 9194
Nearest U: Waterloo
Sauna for men
Open seven days week: 24 hours
Admission: £10
The low lighting and steamy
atmosphere makes everyone far
more attractive than they really
are. Quite a good place to meet new
'friends', and chill out.

Pleasuredrome North
278 Calendonian Road
Tel: 0171 607 0063
Nearest U: Kings Cross
Open Mon-Thu 12noon-1am;
Fri-through to Mon 1am
Admission: £10
A gay sauna for men only.

Gay Escorts

Capital Escorts
Male escorts for men.
Telephone: 0171 630 7567.
All major credit cards accepted.
Exclusive agency which is friendly,
professional and totally discreet.
Educated, well- presented young
escorts and masseurs. Hotel/home
visits, dinner/theatre evenings,
sightseeing, weekends or longer.
Visit our central London office to
see our outstanding portfolio

Significant Others
14 South Molton Street W1
Tel 0171 499 5939
This is a bureau for professional gay
men charging an annual fee of £450
and as many introductions as it takes
to form a long term relationship
within that period.

Helplines

London Lesbian & Gay Switchboard	Tel: 0171 837 7324
Bisexual Helpline Tue & Wed 7.30pm-9.30pm	Tel: 0181 569 7500
Black Lesbian & Gay Helpline	Tel: 0171 837 5364
Glad Legal Advice	Tel: 0171 251 6911
National Aids Helpline	Tel: 0800 567 123
The Terrence Higgins Trust 12noon-10pm daily	Tel: 0171 242 1010
London Friend (for coming out)	Tel: 0171 837 3337
London Lesbian& Gay Teenage Group	Tel: 0171 263 5932
Health and Aids Crusaid	Tel: 0171 834 7566
GMFA	Tel: 0171 738 3712
PRESSURE GROUPS Outrage!	Tel: 0171 439 2381
Stonewall Group	Tel: 0171 222 9007

Stag & Hen Nights

Stag nights seem to date from the time of Henry VIII, when it was quite normal for a group of young knaves, one of whom was to be married the next day, to go on a wild drinking spree, visiting a variety of houses of ill repute, uprooting horse carts and generally causing mayhem along the way. This was considered fitting recompense for the 'sacrifice' which the 'unfortunate' fella was due to make in the morning. Any young man not leaving a trail of wreckage behind him was considered to be "tempting the fates" to restore him his freedom one day and, what is more, somewhat less than "a man my son."

Hen nights are a much more recent phenomenon, and were little heard of before the 60's. They arose as a quite justified "you're getting yours so I'm going to make damned sure that I get mine"- type reaction to stag nights.

Girls Night Out

If you'd like to rival the knaves of the past in the excitement stakes consider starting your evening by splashing out on a night-time helicopter tour of London. Surveying your, as yet unconquered/ never to be conquered dominions from 1000 feet is truly breathtaking, and works out at only £30 each for a twenty minute tour. Speak to Skyline helicopters about their four- seater Robson R22 helicopters, which can pick you up and set you down in Docklands. The feeling is one of profound freedom and heightened sense aware-ness. So, even though you've by-passed the Chippendales, you won't have sacrificed much, with the thrill of a chopper at hand.

Panoramic views of London can be enjoyed from 'Windows ' in the Hilton Hotel Park Lane

The food delivers what the mouth watering aroma wafting out of the kitchen promises. Meals aren't exclusively Thai, but a Mexican/ Thai barbecue is available. A function room is at your disposal downstairs and the staff are quite prepared to provide the music, and to stay open as late as you wish.

Boys Night Out

Guys, why not survey your unconquered dominions in real style. If you're prepared to splash out somewhat for this special night then you wont beat Windows at the top of the Hilton Hotel in Park Lane. Everything is in place to enable you to eat like kings.

The view is absolutely mesmerising, and the exciting live band will encourage even the most timid of you up on the dance floor. A fixed price, five course dinner will cost you around £45. As a saucy alternative why not try "School Dinners' near Baker Street. The delectable school uniform-attired waitresses are sure to tickle your fancy - and that's not all. Another good way of spending a stag

night out is paintballing. The cost is around £40 and you will be provided with goggles, a gun, pellets and food. For maximum enjoyment it is well worth making up your own group which involves about twenty people.

LA Stretch Limo Service
36 Ravenswood Road E17
Tel: 0181 923 9988
This is a very popular Stretch Limo Service operating 24 hours a day. For a five hour ride through the nocturnal streets of London in this white dream machine it will cost you and your friends a mere £295. Inside the curved seats, lunch box sized TV. and rows of glasses promise a cocktail-filled life

School Dinners
1 Robert Adam St.(Off Baker St.) W1
Tel: 0171 486 2724
A long time favourite with the Stag and Hen crowd; and according to the owners it is as well known as the Ritz, Harrods and Planet Hollywood. So if you want to be forced fed with custard pie and spanked by the St. Trinian clad girls this is definitely the place for you.

LA Stretch Limo Service: Paul Westford's dream-machine; the ideal way to travel around the streets of London

Go Karting

Go Karting
Formula 1 Chelsea SW6
191 Townsmead Road
Tel: 0171 371 0202
A 300m circuit on the site of a
converted warehouse close to
Chelsea Harbour offers a wide
variety of entertainment complete
with tunnels, bank curves and
electronic scoreboard.

Motor Racing

Brands Hatch
Fawkham Longfield Kent
Tel: 0171 01474 872331
If you fancy emulating the feats of
your favourite racing driver, now is
your big opportunity. At Brands Hatch
you can join the racing/ four wheel
drive school or go karting. All are
available here for your pleasure. You
can also receive early driving tuition if
you are under seventeen.

Dog Racing

Wembley Stadium
Empire Way Middlesex.
Tel: 0181 902 8833
Restaurant 220 seats. Table d'hote
Racing Mon, Wed and Fri at 7.30pm.
Dine in luxury: first class food,
licensed bars, full ranges of beers and
spirits and a wine list second to none.
TV monitors and great service.
Fully air conditioned and unlimited
parking.

Trains

The Orient Express
Orient Express Victoria SW1
Tel: 0171 620 0003
For your own magical mystery tour,
you can be transported anywhere in
the UK in the famous carriages.
Popular destinations are Leeds Castle
in Kent, and York.

Boats

El Barco Latino
Temple Pier Victoria Embankment WC2
Tel: 0171 379 5496.
Mon-Sat, 12noon-3am; Sun 12noon-
12midnight.
A floating vessel with a Latin
American theme. Fluid fashionable
bar attracting lively, well- dressed
crowd.

Planes

Concorde
Mr Graham Butler,
British Airways, Heathrow Airport
Tel: 0181 513 0202
For all destinations in the world
contact Mr Graham Butler with your
individual chartering requirements of
Concorde. The prices start at around
£500 a head and will take you and
ninety nine of your colleagues and
very close friends for a lunch to
remember, lasting approximately
ninety minutes and reaching
supersonic speeds.

Paintballing

Electrowerkz Two
7 Torrens Street EC1
Tel: 0171 837 6419
This paintball site is set in 30,000 sq. feet of converted warehouse in Islington. Ideal place to have some fun if you have three or five hours to kill but you must be over sixteen.

Ballooning

Balloon Safaris
27 Rosefield Rd Staines Middlesex.
Tel: 01784 451007
If you want to team up with a party of 10 or 16 you can go ballooning for the day. Flights are dictated by the weather so having booked, one would need to phone in advance to be advised of the conditions. Most flights take place over the home counties and last about one hour. The cost, £125 (approx.) per person. At the end of your adventure you are offered champagne, photographed and presented with a certificate to mark your achievement.

Helicopters

Skyline Helicopters
Wycombe Air Park Nr Marlow Bucks
Tel: 01494 451111
The four seater Robson R44 will cost you about £30 each for a twenty minute night time tour. The feeling is one of profound freedom and will take you one thousand feet above the ground before setting you down in Docklands.

School Dinners: A long established venue for stag and hen nights

Venues

Anemos
32 Charlotte Street W1
Tel: 0171 636 2289

A well rehearsed song would be in order when you visit this long time favourite haunt for girls about to take the plunge. The food is instantly forgettable but the smashing and jovial atmosphere should ring in your ear long after the night is over.

Aquarium
260 Old Street ECI
Tel: 0171 729 9779.

Wet 'N' Wild: The best of British beef with The Dreamboys, every Friday at the club with the pool on stage where the boys cavort and where ladies can join them in the pool or in a warm Jacuzzi. Thank Funk It's Friday, the '70s & '80s club night is between, 10pm-4am, and £15 for access to the intimate 'dream on' lounge.

Nikita's Russian Restaurant
65 Ifield Road SW10
Tel: 0171 352 6326
Open 7.30-12 midnight
Four Private party rooms

You have a choice of twenty different Russian and Polish vodkas at this eaterie. Taped Russian background music sets the mood to the swashbuckling rip-roaring atmosphere. Classic Russian dishes comprise caviar, blinis, beefstroganoff and filet Leningrad. One word of warning, if you do not know your vodka could leave here in a very sorry state indeed.

The Male Strip Saloon
Walker's Court Brewer Street W1
Tel: 0171 734 1593

Show every Saturday at 10pm, Bar open from 9pm. Reserved seats £10 The Male Strip Saloon has the same entrance as the Raymond Revuebar. and offers the 'full monty' A fun night out for the ladies, an all male nude revue with the most masculine men at their muscular, raunchy, wicked best and baring it all!

Downtown
Odessa Street Rotherhithe SE16
Tel: 0171 231 8838

This is a very popular venue with the 'girlies'. The cabaret is titled 'Girls Night Out' and features Physique the handsome hunk. On Thursday and Friday nights they offer an all inclusive package for around £35 that includes a four course meal,drinks, live cabaret and DJ.

Venues and Services

Awesome Events
Tel: 0171 233 5557
One of the leading party crews in organizing product launches, summer balls,stag and hen nights. If you need an incentive - the organizer qualifies for a weekend break.

The Party Bus
Vigilant House
120 Wilton Road Victoria SW1
Tel: 0171 630 6063 Fax: 0171 233 8474
E-Mail: denis@partyexpress.co.uk
The Party Bus is a traditional red double-decker bus with a difference. It is fully equipped with all the latest PA and CD sound systems and decorated with balloons and streamers. For the price of your ticket you will be able to visit four of London's top nightclubs in one evening and the only extra money that you may have to spend is over the bar.

Thai Buffalo
561 Garratt Lane SW18
Tel: 0181 944 7617
Will offer you pavement tables and a garden barbecue at Bàr 366 (its wine bar offshoot is just a little further down the road). The food is absolutely mouth-watering and well worth considering.

Murder Mystery Dinner Theatre
Tel: 0171 402 4161 for details
At the following venues:
Raddison Hotel Tottenham Court Road.
Forte Hotel Regents Park.
New Connaught Rooms Holborn
The Ambassadors Hotel Bloomsbury.
The Rembrandt South Kensington.
If you want to put your powers of detection to the test, you will find your evening both entertaining and intriguing. You get a three course meal, three murders and a DJ.

Good Times at Cairo Jacks
10 Beak Street
Near Piccadilly Circus W1
Call the hotline for group bookings and other information
Tel: 0181 906 9921
Billed as London's number one 70's and 80's club. This can be a pretty crazy venue on Friday and Saturday nights. They seem to get their fair quota of hen nights, and office leaving bashes where anything goes.

Break For the Border
8 Argyll Street Oxford Circus W1
Tel: 0171 734 5776
Open: Mon-Wed; 5pm- till late Thurs-Sats 5pm-3am
Happy hour daily between 5pm-7pm
Chill out at Break For The Border where you will get a free round of Margaritas with your meal.

Villa Stefano
227 High Holborn WC1
Tel: 0181 343 7808
Open: Lunch 12noon - 4pm
Dinner: 5.30 - 2am
Dance the night away with the aid of a superb sound system and resident DJ.

Table Dancing

Between the brogue-shod feet of a City businessman, a naked girl is on her hands and knees looking for her knickers.

Where have they got to wails 19 year old Cara, struggling to make herself heard over the music. She had discarded the thong with feigned carelessness - only minutes earlier. The businessman, a bespectacled thirtysomething in a crisp black suit does not flinch. In fact he is thoroughly enjoying the experience - snarling conspiratorially behind her back to the amusement of his colleagues.

This is the bizzare world of lap-dancing/tableside dancing/striptease, call it what you will. Three years ago these middle-class men would never have dreamed of being here. Now however, a night out at a lap-dancing club is positively fashionable. It has been given a respectability by the involvement of big businessmen and, crucially, the patronage of celebrities. Golfer Tiger Woods is one, film star Nicolas Cage another. He visited Stringfellows when he was in London; enjoying the attentions of several lap-dancers. Remarkably the list of lap-dancing fans include many women. Model Sophie Dahl. All Saints singer, Melanie Blatt, actress Sadie Frost and Yasmin Le Bon.

Only three years ago, there was no such thing as lap-dancing in Britain. Now there are reckoned to about two hundred clubs where men pay young women to stand inches (by law three feet) from their faces - and strip. This strangely impersonal spectacle lasts the duration of a pop song, after which the man will pay the young woman between £10 and £20. She will then move on in search of a another customer. and he will wait to be attended by another dancer.

It may seem that lap-dancing is stripping repackaged for the nineties. And indeed it is. Now stripping is lap-dancing and it is no longer shameful - respectable leisure companies are taking an interest in the clubs.

They are after a slice of the lucrative corporate entertainment market - businessmen on expense accounts.

The perfect moment. at For Your Eyes Only

The Windmill
International

**London's Premier Tableside Dancing Club
with 75 Beautiful Dancing Girls
who will perform tableside for you.
Full nudity-continuous stage show**

V.I.P Bar and Balcony

Games Room - Valet Parking

V.I.P. Bar is available for private hire

The Windmill
International

OPEN MONDAY-SATURDAY 8.30pm-3.30am

Dress: Smart

Tel: 0171 439 3558/9 Fax: 0171 287 2972
The Windmill is located just off Piccadilly Circus
**17-19 Great Windmill Street
London W1 7PH**

Lap - dancing came from America. There, it is a £5 billion industry. Few expected this brash entertainment to catch on here. It gained a foothold in Britain when Peter Stringfellow persuaded magistrates to grant him a license to open 'Cabaret of Angels' at his eponymous London nightclub. It was the beginning of an unlikely trend.

The lap-dancers can earn up to £1,000 a week. Typically, they will pay the club £50 for the right to work, then everything they earn is theirs. The clubs make their money from entrance fees, drinks and food.

At another club I spotted Cara struggling to retrieve her knickers from underneath a businessman. Everywhere you look, taut young female flesh, lightly bronzed, is cavorting in front of pallid middle-aged businessmen .

Cara, who is training to become an actress, eventually locates her under - wear, which she threads awkwardly over her glittering stilettos. She graciously accepts a folded brown bank note from her customer. He is rewarded with a chaste peck on the cheek. It is the only physical contact of their encounter, and it is also the only time

he looks Cara in the eyes. His gaze was previously fixed elsewhere. Some commentators have described lap-dancing as a blow for feminism; the theory being that if men are stupid enough to part with their money the girls should be free to take it off them. Some of the strippers have children, others are students, supplementing their grants. Many are failed dancers There is certainly no shortage of women wanting the work. At the clubs I visited they descended ravenously on the tables of men at the end of every song. Some made conversation first. Others just said; 'can I dance for you'.? Some of the men took this as a sign that the girls enjoyed their work. But only a fool could conclude that the avidity of the girls' interest is anything but mercenary.

The Mayfair Club

15 Berkeley Street W1
Tel: 0171 0171 629 0010
Open: Mon-Sat 7pm -2am
New, unique and exclusive membership only club in the heart of Mayfair. Serving excellent cuisine with entertainment by the Mayfair Babes, 100 beautiful girls providing the best in cabaret- style table dancing. Modelled on the original American club concept, it offers stylish surroundings, luxurious bars and restaurants including private dining rooms serving modern cuisine. Media facilities include Reuter's, Bloomberg e-mail and satellite. You have a choice: you can apply for either private or corporate membership.

Cabaret of Angels

16-19 St Martin's Lane WC2
Tel: 0171 240 5534
Entrance £10 before 10pm otherwise £15 (no membership required)
Mon-Thu 7pm-3.30am
Lap dancing seemed to became popular and respectable in London when Peter Stringfellow persuaded magistrates to grant him a license to open at his eponymous London nightclub. and he is now hosting table-side-dancing at his club four nights a week.

Chaplins Table Dancing

9 Swallow Street, W1.
Tel: 0171 287 1056
Open 8.30pm-3.30am.
Entrance £10 (no membership)
Table dancing was introduced to London six years ago by this club, and is now a firm favourite with the stag night crowd. Sexy girl dancers are in constant action on the half - pint sized-dance-floor and a quick nod or a wink will bring the girl to your table, where she will continue to dance specifically for your enjoyment.

For Your Eyes Only

Abbey Road, Park Royal NW10.
Tel: 0181 965 7699/020-8965-7699
Open Monday to Saturday until 3am.
A totally fun and fantasy experience! The ultimate adult entertainment-tableside dancing at its very best in friendly, comfortable surroundings. For Yours Eyes Only features a host of stunning dancers who, if invited, will dance totally nude at a customer's table for a standard tip of £10 per record track. The club operates strict house rules and provides the highest standards of service. It caters for all occasions,from special stag party packages, through to corporate and fine dining facilities. Admission is £20 and £10 is returned to you by way of food and drink vouchers. Book one of FYEO'S exclusive VIP suites to entertain guests in style (different admission charges apply). Full bar and food menus are served at realistic prices. For Your Eyes Only also has clubs in Bournemouth and Southampton. Over 20's only. Smart casual dress. Strict house rules always apply. Call for an information pack.

Cherokee Club

43 45 East Smithfield, El.
Tel: 0171 702 3300.
Open Mon Fri noon midnight.
Tower Hill Tower Gateway DLR)
This City club offers 'entertainment', a restaurant and ok food. A relaxing

Full of close-up confidence at For Your Eyes only

bar and service by attractive staff, The dancers move rather seductively to the music but are only allowed to remove their 'bra'- which leaves quite a lot to the imagination.

Secrets
62 Glenthorne Rd; Hammersmith W6
Tel: 0181 563 0652
Also at: 309 Finchley Road NW3
Tel: 0171 794 1267
Mon-Fri 7pm-2am; Sat 8pm-2am
Dress Code: Smart/casual
Entrance £5 per person before 8pm and £15 after 8pm
It is no secret that this club attracted a great deal of publicity when it first opened its doors in this quite residential street in West London.

Here you get the up-close and personal treatment at this small, but very compact venue. The dancers invite their 'ten pounder', to take a seat by the stage and they in turn perform a very erotic dance at eye level for the duration of a record track The club is now run by the Drameh sisters, Joy and Jill (not nuns) who seem to have created an extra buzz about the place since our last visit. They have also branched out by opening Secrets 2 in Finchley Road in North London; and after a slow start are beginning to turn things around - but it will have to go along way to capture the atmosphere of the Hammersmith venue.

Venus

29 /35 Farringdon Road EC1

U: Farringdon

Open Mon-Fri 5pm-3am Sat 8pm-3am

Fully air conditioned

This is London's latest and most laid-back dancing club situated in the heart of the city. Set in comfortable surroundings with a relaxing bar, with full a la carte menu available and prompt service by attractive and courteous staff. Upon request the most stunning beauties from around the world perform fully nude erotic dancing at your table while you relax and enjoy a truly breathtaking treat.

Sophisticats at Volante House

1 Marylebone Lane, Wl.

Junction of Henrietta Place

Tel: 0181 201 8804 Daytime: or

0171 224 4488 Evenings:

U: Bond Street; Open Mon- Thurs 7.30 - 3.30am Showtime; Feline Rhapsody at 10.30pm Les Tigress at midnight.

The only private members club in Europe to offer a glamourous, nude cabaret stage show and table dancing, (nude and topless), cat lap dining, drinks and entertainment all under one roof.

The Windmill

17/19 Great Windmill Street W1

Tel: 0171 439 3558

£10 entrance; Dress Code: Smart Casual American style table- dancing is on offer at this famous residence. With the war time motto of 'we never close' and latterly 'if it moves it's rude' conjures up an extraordinary feeling of nostalgia. Back in the 'raunchy nineties' we are greeted with around 100 girls who strut around this magnificent old theatre and will dance for you, at your table for a mere £10 tip. The girls are completely nude and we can see this venue becoming extremely popular mainly because of its location and history.

Fetish

"You can tell novices by the way they tie their knots. Sometimes people get cramps and soreness and someone has to step in to assist. Everyone is really helpful here and looks out for everyone else", says a Saturday nighter at Club Fantastic Masked Ball.

Over in the corner by the bar a middle-aged man is licking a woman's patent leather-boots while she orders him to look up. Another man is being led away from the dance floor on a leash. He's all obedience and appreciative looks. The scene and the music may be like any other club. The dance floor is a seething mass of gyrating bodies but here many of the mixed bunch of people are being, not to put too fine a point on it, tied to pillars or to the wall. Some are being spanked or ritually humiliated by women of all ages: dressed in anything from Lycra shorts with a touch of lace, to a rubber suit sprinkled with metallic studs with matching face mask. When they have finished the recipient of the treatment will often give them a hug and a kiss.

The club runs the gamut of the whole scene, from a simple desire to wear high heels, rubber and leather to cross-dressing and role reversal. But the majority don't seem to be into that. Most are here to have a good time. I think it all starts with a couple of silk scarves and for many it seems to stay like that.

You're completely cut off from normal life here - whatever that is. I was sitting at the bar quite nervously and a middle-aged American man dressed in a little more than a few leather straps said it would give him the greatest pleasure to lick my boots. I thought, 'Wow, that's really cool' I have been in clubs where people are running around completely starkers and I have seen blood drawn by a beating, but by and large you don't get heavy duty action in this club.

In Regency London there were about twenty places that provided pleasures such as spanking, tying up and beating and the Prince Regent himself was thought not to be averse

Our own age has witnessed Cynthia Payne's Streatham bordello for the famous and not-so-famous where, she claimed, some of the highest judges in the land received a full service of spanking and role-play.

When she was brought to court, The Spectator pleaded memorably for tolerance of private acts ' which don't offend or frighten the horses'. In fact, more than half the pleasure is in dressing up. The shopper searching for fetish wear suffers a rather bewildering set of experiences Getting into some shops is, in itself a very hit-and-miss affair, with irregular opening hours. Entry-phones and steely eyed -assistants who presumably want to ensure that only serious shoppers are admitted. In Pagan Ritual I am offered a gold lamé top cut like a cage to expose the chest. I opt instead for a leather waistcoat to go with rubber jeans and just hope
I blend on the night.

Skin Two affords a spectacle of leather and rubber appliances that turn out to be items of clothing. The emphasis is on leather and rubber knobs, spikes and other protuberances. Some articles of clothing seem to consist of little else.

Fetish dressing has also infiltrated mainstream fashion, albeit in attenuated form. No Jean Paul Gaultier outfit would be complete without fetish undertones. But this form of sexual expression is still part of a relatively underground scene. Most clubs can only be contacted through a Post Office box number.

They shift location and close suddenly - all part of the thrill of the hunt for the connoisseur, but also a necessity. Since the police's Operation Spanner in 1990 which resulted in a High Court ruling that consensual acts of sado-masochistic sex in private are illegal, the S/M world has become increasingly secretive. There is also concern over the expansion of the scene over the past couple of years. It used to be a small and intimate scene where you knew virtually everyone, now all sorts of people want to get involved

The owners of Severin's Kiss state that there are people who, although suitably dressed, seem to regard other clubbers as a numourous spectacle. Such people are ejected.

I chat to a relatively staid-looking couple in from the suburbs, it's a habit they have to indulge on the side. 'We just want to come out dress up, and dance together', they say, 'Were not greatly into the sexual side but do like rubber and PVC clothing.' Sonia's attire consists of two thongs in stretch rubber that cross her torso and lunge down to her crotch. 'There's nothing to be shy about with what we do', giggles Sonia, "but I'd never tell anyone that we come here".

CLUB FANTASTIC
is held once a month at The Vox.
Severin's Kiss is held at various venues.
Details can be obtained by phoning:
0891 445 911
or contact: Pagan Ritual: 0171 287 2096
Paradiso Bodyworks: 0171 287 2487
Skin Two: 0181 968 9692
Zeitgeist: 0171 607 2977

Fetish Shops

Ann Summers
155 Charing Cross Road WC2
Tel: 0171 437 1886
This front section of this boutique
style-shop sells lingerie and swim-
wear, and at the back, there is a
display of models in leather and a
colossal range of vibrators, strawberry
nipple drops and a video selection.
They also have a shop in Bayswater
and branches throughout London.

Banned
2 Cross Street Islington N1
Tel: 0171 704 2766
A tiny shop concentrating chiefly on
second hand lingerie. French knickers
from the twenties to more recent
times. Corsetry, satin suspenders and
white cotton bloomers are all in stock.

Clone Zone
64 Old Compton Street W1
Tel: 0171 287 3530
Also: 1 Hogarth Rd Earls Ct SW5
Tel: 0171 373 0598
Through great demand this shop has
now opened-up in Queer Street and
specialises in rubber, leather and
sportswear for men.

Cover Girl
44 Cross Street N1
Tel: 0171 354 2883
Specialising in TV wear, high heeled
shoes and wigs.

East of Eden
519/523 Cambridge Heath E2
Tel: 0171 739 0292

Jo Guest modelling for the Fury Range:
available from Ann Summers

The showroom contains a large
collection of wet-look, lycra, PVC and
leather. A good stock of boots shoes
and wigs are also available

Expectations
75 Great Eastern Street EC2
Tel:0171 739 0292
Specialises in S & M rubber and
leather gear. Most of these items are
hand made to measure on the
premises.

Club R.U.B.
319 City Road EC1
London's latest wildand wicked once a
month venue for those who like to
dress up -or down.

Presiding over the proceedings.

Honour
86 Lower Marsh Waterloo SE1
Tel: 0171 401 8219
Mon-Fri 10.30am-7pm; Sat 11-5pm
Fetish clothing store stocking a wide range of rubber, leather, bondage and PVC wear.

The House of de Sade
8/9 Walkers Court Soho W1
Tel: 0171 437 2349
A fetish store in the hub of Soho. Rubber, leather, PVC, corsets, boots shoes, bondage, magazines & videos.

Libido
83 Parkway NW1
Tel: 0171 485 0414
Specialises in hot clothes ,as well as rubber, leather and PVC .

Pagan Metal
29 Brewer Street W1
Tel: 0171 287 2487

Large stocks of items for men and women, including wigs, boots, accessories, shoes and stilletos in large sizes.

Ritual Shoes
Basement 29 Brewer Street W1
Tel: 0171 287 2096
A wide range of stiletto boots and platform shoes are on sale here, to satisfy all your requirements. The sizes range from 3-12 including half-sizes with 4" or 6" heels.
They also offer a mail order service.

Regulation
17a St Albans Place N1
Tel: 0171 226 0665
For a total refit, including fetters. A highly specialised collection of physical restraint equipment of unrivalled quality and design.

Skin Two
23 Grand Union Centre
Kensal Road W10
Tel: 0181 968 9692
This boutique has a stylish interior and good changing facilities; to light classical music. A vast collection of rubber wear is on display. There are spiked mini-skirts and pocket bras harnessed to panties.

Transformation
50 Eversholt Street NW1
Tel:0171 388 0627
This is an ideal place for transvestites to visit and be completely transformed, with fully trained staff available to advise on make-up and hair, as well as clothes.Voice training is also available if required.

Red Light Areas

Kings Cross
This is the most dangerous notorious area in London with up to four hundred prostitutes literally fighting for clients. The police will be watching you on hidden cameras. It's a rough, tough area. Many of the girls are teenagers on drugs.

It all happens in the depressing streets around King's Cross Station. British Rail operates cheap 'Away Day' fares to London and since so some of these prostitutes now come from out of town they tend to call it- "Have It Away Day".

Many of the girls will pick up a 'punter' on the train to London, service him in the toilet, flog their bodies for five hours and be home in time to have the old man's tea on the table when he gets back from work.

Earls Court. Also known as kangaroo valley, it's full of sexy Aussies. The phone boxes are saturated with cards and the large houses of Earls Court Road all seem to have a token hooker.
There is a gay sex shop across the road from the tube station and, a mere boomerang's throw away is the Coleherne, Britain's most profitable pub, absolutely heaving with leather-clad gay guys all looking incredibly macho in their outfits. It's surprising how many of them, on closer examination, turn out to be rather mild-mannered assistant bank managers. This area is truly cosmo-politan. The people are honestly hedonistic.

Streatham
Forever linked to Cynthia Payne and her hilarious brothel immortalised in the film 'Personal Services'.
It's a leafy suburb which seems an unlikely spot for a vice area but it's been going on for generations. The police are actively in pursuit of the girls and the kerb crawlers. It's a bit like the Keystone Cops at times. The prostitute-hunting police are known as The Tom Squad and you can see it all happening in the area around Tooting Common.

Brixton.
Nearby Streatham is bustling Brixton. It's calmed down a bit since it used to have its regular killings and riots. Railton Road is the base for the many black prostitutes and some white girls. It's certainly cheap but we wouldn't say it's particularly cheerful.

Whitechapel
Across the river in London's East End is also highly avoidable unless you fancy being rearranged a la Jack The Ripper. The working girls, as they are known, are to be found around Commercial Street - which seems very appropriate.

Shepherd's Market

High class whores have aspired to
Shepherd's Market since the year dot.
Back in the 1680's they began the
May Fairs which gave the area its
name and a licentious time was had
by all. Before the Wolfenden Report in
the late fifties the area was stiff with
the most glamourous women in the
world. Now it's all more discreet but
they're still around in the bars,
restaurants and casinos.

Soho

So-Ho ! They used to cry as the
riders chased the foxes across what is
now known as London's wicked
Square mile. The whips cracked then
and the whips crack now.
Now it has more to do with S&M - Le
vice Anglais - isn't it typical of the
French ? One of their lot, The
Marquise de Sade, invents it and
suddenly it's our problem.
The sex industry will always be part
of Soho - half of which is owned by
Paul Raymond, owner of the famous
Revue Bar. The girls still have red
lights in the windows and the cards
on the doors just like the old days :
"Lovely Model. Come upstairs !"
There's a very smart gay scene too
around Old Compton Street. A dildo
throw away is Piccadilly Circus where
the rent boys hang around the
amusement arcades. Many of them
are teenage runaways who have left
home for the bright lights but it
usually ends in tears.

Marble Arch

Welcome to down town Dubai.Do you
buy sex ? Look in any phone box !
 All along the Edgware Road wealthy
Arabs sit outside the all-night cafes
smoking their hookahs (that's the
oriental tobacco-pipe with a long tube
passing through a glass container of
water that cools the smoke as it is
drawn through) and surveying the
hookers. It has been estimated that
there are four thousand working girls
prostituting themselves in London
and a goodly proportion of them are
in this part of town.

Ace Sauna
508 Kings Road SW10
Tel: 0171 352 1370
Open Mon-Fri 11am-1.30am
Sat-Sun 12noon -midnight
Situated in the heart of Chelsea.
This long established sauna also
offers a good massage in very
congenial surroundings.
Complimentary drinks at the bar.

Body One
140 Marylebone Road NW1
Tel: 0171 486 5675
Open Mon-Sun 10am-10pm
Probably one of the most centrally
located saunas of all and within a
'waxworks' of Madame Tussauds.
Here you can enjoy a sauna and
massage and be pampered by one of
the three very attentive masseuses.
The gym is reasonably well equipped,
and the reception you get on arrival is
warm and friendly.

Co-Co's Sun Lounge
& Massage Centre
1037 Finchley Road NW11
Tel: 0181 458 8132
Open Mon- Sun 10am - 11pm
This may be out of the centre of
London but it is well worth the
journey, if you like a genuinely good
massage. The atmosphere is relaxing
and services such as shiatsu,
aromatherapy, sauna, steam room
and jacuzzi are all on offer.

Edgware Unisex Health
& Beauty Centre
96 High Street, Edgware Middlesex
Tel: 0181 952 5952
Open seven days 11am-9pm.
On offer here is massage, steam bath,
body scrub, solarium and beautician.
Despite being quite a distance from
the centre of London if you want a
really good massage,moderately
priced, in unhurried surroundings -
its worth making the trip. They
generally have three attractive
masseuses on duty.

First Class
180 Royal College Street NW1
Tel: 0171 267 4709
Open seven days 11am-5am
U: Camden Town
This establishment is not everything
that the name suggests. In darkest
Camden Town you will find at least
seven girls in attendance most
evenings. The masseuses are of
varying ages but all are between
twenty and thirty. The shower offered
erratic impulse and the sauna was
cold - even though it seemed to be a
glorified excuse to lull you into a
feeling that you have had value for
money.

New Experience
275 Eversholt Street, NWI.
Tel: 0171 387 6441
Near Mornington Crescent tube
(Opposite Camden Palace).
Take your choice from discreet multi
national masseuses. Totally refurbished with sun bed and V.I.P.
room (en suite) , complimentary
refreshments in the TV lounge area.

Sauna & Massage

Omega Health Club
141 145 Kentish Town Road, NWI.
Tel: 0171 482 5538
Open seven days.
Well laid out, large, modern, new sauna with private massage rooms. Friendly, relaxing atmosphere and free light refreshments. Bar and TV lounge.

Rainbow Health & Beauty
428 Edgware Road W2.
Tel: 0171 402 6499
U: Edgware Road
Open daily 12.30pm 10pm.
Genuine massage, hot bubble bath, private rooms, free refreshments and a varied selection of Eastern European ladies to pamper you

Rio's Mixed Sauna Club
241 Kentish Town Road NW5
Tel: 0171 485 0607
Mon-Sat 11am -7am
Sat couples only 8pm-12midnight
Sun 11am/10pm
Nearest U: /BR Kentish Town
Relax in 3000 square feet of tropical surroundings. Two large jaccuzis, steam room, sauna,plunge pool, large TV lounge. Nudity optional.

Swiss Cottage Sauna
2 New College Parade
Finchley Road NW6
Tel: 0171 586 4422
24 hours a day 365 days a year.
One of the longest established saunas and massage parlours in London

Strand Health Club
Savoy Courtyard 96 Strand WC2.
Tel: 0171 497 8950
Open 7days a week: Mon Fri
7am 3am: Sat & Sun 12-3am.
Exclusively located health club with luxury lounge area and relaxed surroundings. The most prestigious service offered is traditional Thai massage performed by fully qualified therapists. The Club offers a fully-equipped fitness suite in a friendly and non-competitive environment.

The Lanacombe Sauna
70 Crouch End Hill Hornsey N8
Tel: 0181 340 4677
Open Mon-Sat 11am-midnight;
Sun 2pm-midnight
What is particularly striking about this place is when you enter through the main door you are immediately confronted by at least seven masseuses who lounge around the reception area. Despite the in-your-face treatment and basic facilities, the girls are generally attractive and the massage is pretty good.

The 109 Club
109 Shoreditch High Street, El.
Tel: 0171 613 5301
Liverpool Street Station
Offering a new executive concept in sauna and massage in a luxurious health club atmosphere. Total choice of twenty masseuses.Relaxing lounge with waitress service for sandwiches and light refreshments. Six comfortable rooms, VIP sauna and lounge. Open seven days, noon till late.

Massage

Australian Blonde
Beautiful, warm and friendly
Australian blonde masseuse will relax
and pamper you in her luxury,
centrally - located Baker Street home.
Telephone Sandy on 0171 935 2525

Amy
Danger!! Totally addictive and
absolutely stunning. Very friendly
(you wont get better). Luxury
apartment. Tel: 07000 955 955

Dark and Lovely
Tall slim ex-glamour model with a
shapely busty figure will spoil you in
her luxury flat in the SW1 area.
Tel: 0171 976 6271
Mobile: 0956 957540

In Strictest Confidence
London's best selection of ladies.
Theatre and dinner companions.
Home and and hotel visiting.
Our promise is your enjoyment.
Talk with our ladies now on a one to
one 0171 263 1313 CC's. 24 hours.
Visit us on our web site:
www.escortsinternational.co.uk

New Exclusive Babes
The finest and friendliest Masseuses
in Central London. From Asian,
Persian, Oriental and Continental
offer first class service for gentlemen
who require the best. Phone: 0956
223317 Credit cards welcome. 24hrs

Relaxation
And pleasure in delightful
surroundings to deliver a feeling of
well-being and enchantment.Call
Claudia 07000 783 933. SW1 Area

Stunning
Stunning masseuse very friendly and
discreet can entertain you at her
luxurious apartment or your
hotel.room.. Call anytime on 0171 589
6444 CC's accepted.

Massage

Russian Delight
Beautiful and classy brunette offers
sensual massage for ladies and
gentlemen. VIP services Hotel/ home
visits. All CCs' accepted. Telephone:
0171 565 8336 Mobile: 07930 881424

Sally
Stunning and shapely blue -eyed
blonde to tease and tantalize in a
luxurious apartment. Videos, drinks
and showers. Baker Street.Telephone:
0171 224 2444

Sensual Blonde
25 years old. half Brazilian/half
Swedish beauty, offers a relaxing
massage in her luxury Knightsbridge
apartment. Appointments only for
Home and Hotel visits. CC's welcome.
Tel: 0171 584 0761

Tania
Sensual brunette with a sparkling
personality offers a superb massage in
her cozy Chelsea apartment or can
visit you in your home or hotel.Phone
anytime 0171 536 9165 CC.s welcome

Escort Agencies

The Direct Contact
Visiting Escort Service
Park Lane W1
Tel: 0171 584 4447
Confidential, reliable and discreet.
You can choose having spoken to one
of our most beautiful girls from
around the world.

Kensington Playboy Escorts
10a Kensington Church Street W8
Tel: 0171 937 9133
Open daily from 3pm-12 midnight

Portman Escorts
67 Chiltern Stréet W1
Tel: 0171 486 3724
Open daily from 3pm-12midnight

Taj Mahal
Exclusive selection of beautiful high
class escorts of Indian, Persian, Asian,
Oriental and Continental. For VIP
gentlemen who prefer the best.
Telephone 0956 233317
Most cc's welcome. 24 hours.

Escort Agencies

Aristocats
3 Shouldham Street W1
Visit us and choose from a wide
selection of international girls or
simply phone 0171 258 0090

Capital Escorts
Male escorts for men.
Exclusive agency which is friendly,
professional and totally discreet.
Educated, well-presented young
escorts and masseurs. Hotel/home
visits, dinner/theatre evenings,
sightseeing, weekends or longer.
Visit our central London office to
see our outstanding portfolio or
Telephone: 0171 630 7567.
All major credit cards accepted.

Chelsea Girl Escorts
Agency established 26 years
Come and visit our attractive girls
and choose your escort for the
evening. The girls are at 51
Beauchamp Place Knightsbridge
from 7.30pm until 2am Telephone:
0171 584 2749 or 0171 584 6513

Direct Link Escorts
The Free Introduction Agency
Lots and lots of lovely ladies for all
occasions. Hotel visiting.Telephone
Clarissa now on 0171 833 9955 or
0171 263 1313. Major Credit Cards
accepted. 24 hours.Visit our web site:
www.escortsinternational.co.uk

Bill Glen's & Adams of Mayfair
(Established in.1976 by Bill Glen)
"The country's most exclusive escort
agency" - Business Age. Also featured in
The Times Magazine, London
Weekend Television, the BBC's 'Money
Programme and Anglia Television. Let
our ladies and guys introduce
themselves! on
09063 666565 (24 hours) with unique
replay facility up-dated weekly.
Cost 60pence per minute at all times.
PGA Box 5306 WC1N 3XX
Bookings (10am-2am) daily.
0171 706 2607 or 0850 469255
For la crème de la crème only! CCs.
Vacancies for London and Nationwide.
Visit our website:www.billglens.com

Private Escorts

Angel Escorts
The professional exclusive and discreet escort service. Friendly young ladies from around the globe who are both gentle and fun to be with.
Tel: 07050 202 766 (CC's 24hours.)

Charming Escort
Glamourous, chic, elegant and exclusive top escort available for fun night out/in: Tel:0171 584 4447.

Black Beauty Escort Service
Elegant, educated and friendly. Exclusively selective and discreet. Perfect companion for all occasions. Telephone: 0181 203 9637. Visiting Service. Credit Cards welcome.

Central Escorts
One of London's top escorts. Asian, European Mediterranean and Continental. Classy stunning babes. Telephone 0171 724 2514. CC's 24hrs.

Exclusive
Top exclusive attractive French and Italian lady.Well educated and chic dresser available to accompany you for dinner dates and escort you on special occasions. VIP's only. Prepared to travel Internationally. Telephone: +44(0)1 07747 776947.

Supreme
Exquisite, exotic brunette masseuse, with great figure awaits to fulfil your dreams in luxury Chelsea apartment. Also visits. 24 hours Telephone: 0171 589 6444. CC"s welcome.

After the Party's Over

London's eating habits are becoming more continental. There are more and more establishments serving food and drink into the small hours than ever before making a late night three in the morning.

According to Somerset Maugham, it's always been possible to eat as well in England as anywhere else in the world provided you stick to breakfast three times a day. Perhaps this is the reason places like Vingt Quatre among others, serve breakfast around the clock. Here you will find yourself among kindred spirits.

Many a new relationship has been born at these early morning gatherings. After all you know you're among friends - the only thing you don't have in common is that you've been to different parties and that's a problem that can be put right the next night.

After the party's over is an excellent time to experience old London at her slumbering best and you'll find you are not alone on a fine evening. Take a stroll around London town, see all the famous buildings shimmering in the moonlight.

Visit Covent Garden? Well, it's still magical in the wee small hours, but if you want to experience all the hustle of bustle of the authentic fruit and vegetable market and watch the characters who run London's finest greengrocery establishments, as they vie for the finest and the freshest, then make your way to New Covent Garden in Vauxhall. It's worth it for all the jocular banter.

If you want to enjoy the fragrant atmosphere of your favourite flower shop multiplied a thousand fold you must visit the flower market. It's open from 4am but do try and get there before 8am to find that some thing special for your fair lady. Having worked up a thirst you may notice an exodus at about 5am. This is when people in the know go to the Barley Mow pub on the first floor. Across the town there are a host of late night places catering for the up-all-nighters.

Vingt Quatre : Formerly known as Up-All-Night

Restaurants

Boardwalk
18 Greek Street W1
Tel: 0171 287 2051
Mon-Fri 12noon-3am; Sat 6pm-3am
Trendy meeting place with a
cosmopolitan atmosphere, waterfall
on lower ground floor, two bars.
American - style food served all day.

Mr Kong
21 Lisle Street Wl
Tel: 0171 437 7341
Open daily to 2am
Three floors of Cantonese excellence.
The chef is Mr Kong himself and is
one of the best in Chinatown.

Yungs
23 Wardour Street W1
Tel: 0171-437 4986 Daily to 4am
Well thought of Cantonese
restaurant specialising in sea food
dishes; menu lists over 200 meals.

Lido
41 Gerrard Street W1
Tel: 0171 437 4431
Open daily from 11.30am-4.30am
Extremely busy with fantastically
cheap Cantonese dishes always on
offer- such as the roasted meats and
baked crab.

The Mayflower
68-70 Shaftesbury Avenue W1
Tel: 0171 734 9207
Open daily 12noon-4am
Cantonese specialities are on the
menu in incredible profusion.
Sample the crispy ducks and
crystal prawns.

Hodja Nasreddin
53 Newington Green N1
Tel: 0171 226 7757
Sun-Thu 2am; Fri-Sat to 4am.
Great Turkish restaurant - try the
first floor where it's like dining in a
tent.

Crescent Lounge
Kensington Hilton
79 Holland Park Avenue W11
Tel: 0171 603 3355
Open daily 24 hours, licensed to
1am; Sunday 11pm
Piano, jazz and cocktails can see you
through the night but a little bit on
the expensive side.

24 Hour Shops

Airey Bargain Store
73 Willesden Lane NW10
Tel: 0171 624 5888
Probably the original 24 hour shop
in London. Opened in 1960 by
Hensley Airey, the Jamaican-born
owner, sometimes successfully
managed to exploit a loophole in the
law by staying open around the
clock by selling only to the trade. He
still runs this amazing grocery shop
along the same lines, but the
licensing laws are a little more
relaxed these days.

Harts the Grocer
87 Gloucester Road SW7
Tel: 0171 370 5487
The 24 hour supermarket selling
everything from Dime Bars to prime
fillet steak.They have a total of 80
shops in the chain but only six (at
present) stay open 24 hours.

24 Hour Shops

Riteway
57 Edgware Road W2
Tel: 0171 402 5491
Open 24 hours a day.
Caters for the needs of all the locals.
Lots of fresh fruit, excellent dates and
the cheapest pitta bread in town. This
is where the working girls buy their
snacks and ciggies.

B2
Praed Street Paddington W2
Tel: 0171 402 3117
Warwick Way Victoria SW1
Tel: 0171 630 1510
Westbourne Grove Bayswater W2
Tel: 0171 727 6342
Formerly known as Seven Eleven,
this corner convenience chain of mini
super- markets is really burgeoning,
which shows they must have got it
right. They are open 24 hours a day
and have over fifty branches in and
around Central London .They ain't
cut-price but if you are desperate for
cocoa, Cosmopolitan, cat food or
condoms join the midnight queue.

Best of Food and Wine
35 Charing Cross Road W.C2
Tel: 0171 930 5639
This shop has been operating, very
successfully, 24 hours for the past few
years. A vast selection of wines,
miniatures and beers can be
purchased during normal pub hours.
Newspapers, magazines and a variety
of other goodies are available.

Buy Best
75/77 Charing Cross Road WC2
Tel: 0171 437 4793
Also has a fine delicatessen that sells
sandwiches and other goodies.

Portland Food and Wine
246 -248 Great Portland Street W1
Tel: 0171 387 4772
This is the prime shop in the group of
four operating 24 hours, and is
conveniently situated next to Great
Portland Street underground. The
staff here are extremely helpful even
though they never seem to sleep. We
have called at various times of day
and night and still found the same
cheery assistants.

Breakfast

Fox and Anchor

115 Charterhouse Street EC1
Tel: 0171 253 4838
Mon-Fri 7am -9 pm;
Sat 8am.-10.30 pm.
If, perchance, you wind up in the environs of Smithfield's famous meat market you can have a hearty breakfast and a foaming pint of ale to wash it down, as they've been doing for centuries. Call in advance to book your table for breakfast.

Café Pelican

45 St. Martin's Lane WC2
Tel: 0171 379 0309
Mon- Sat 1am-1.30am-
last orders 12.30am
Impressive brasserie and good early morning venue for breakfast.

Tinseltown

St John's Street EC1
Tel: 0171 689 2424
Snacks all day, breakfasts all night

Buscot Dairy Cafe

44a Harrowby Street W1
Tel: 0171 723 3504
Mon-Fri 6.30 am -4pm
Sat 7am-12.30pm; Closed Sunday
This bustling little cafe has been providing excellent breakfasts for almost thirty years. Most mornings you can rub shoulders with millionaires who have lost fortunes in the nearby gambling casino, taxi drivers, builders and ladies of the night on their way home.

Peter's

59 Pimlico Road SW1
Tel: 0171 730 5991
Open 7am Mon-Sat 8am-10pm
This is an up-market caff for cabbies both in menu and decor. The green faced glass front looks on to leafy Pimlico. The regular clientele seem to be more interested in quantity rather than quality but nevertheless it has survived almost forty years and still offers extremely good value.

Papisseria Cappuccetto

9 Moor Street
Regent Street W1
Tel: 0171 437 9472
Open daily 9am-7pm
Here they serve fresh fruit juice, and wonderful croissants freshly baked on the premises.

Pierre Péchon

127 Queensway W2
Tel: 0171 229 0746
Open Mon Wed 7am -7pm;
Thu 7am-8pm; -Sun 7.30am -7pm
If you want to taste a little bit of France first thing in the morning in cosmopolitan Bayswater, try this long established and excellent patisserie for breakfast. The staff are extremely courteous and efficient, and despite the early morning hustle and bustle seem to balance their attentions between the take-away customers and the leisurely breakfast clientele in the restaurant, with relative ease.

Liquid Breakfast

Railway Tavern
131 Angel Lane E15
Tel: 0181 534 3123
Mon-Sat 6am- 8am-11am -11pm
Night shift workers and clubbers
briefly rub shoulders before going to
work and boogie. Breakfast is
available on request but most
prefer the liquid variety.

Market Tavern
Market Towers
1 Nine Elms Lane SW8
Tel: 0171 622 5655
Open 6am- 8am and 10pm-4am
Mixed crowd during the week and
predominantly gay at weekends.
Breakfast for Covent Garden
market traders only.

Havana Bar
490 Fulham Broadway, SW6
Telephone: 0171 381 5005;
Mon-Sat 5pm-2am, Sun 5pm-12
(also at 17 Hanover Square)

Late Night

Live music Fri. & Sat. South
American sounds including
Merengue. Dance classes Mon (free)
& Thurs (£4). Sunday chill-out with
Brazilian live band. Hand-rolled
cigars sold at the bar.

Dallas
93 Charterhouse Street EC1
Open:Fri and Sun 11pm-7am
Sat 11pm-5am
Heavy duty cholesterol for
Smithfield types. Say no more.

Bar Italia
22 Frith Street, London, Wl
Tel: 0171 437 4520
Open 7 days a week: 24 hours a day
A long time haven for the Soho
habitués and for people looking for
excellent savoury snacks, continental
breakfasts, panini, plus the superb
cappucino and espresso and all this
at any time of the day or night.

The Atlantic Bar & Grill: A Long time favourite with the late nighters

Late Late Night

Café Bohéme
13 Old Compton Street W1
Tel: 0171 734 0623
Right in the heart of Soho, this
popular bar has a license until 3am
but does charge an admission fee
from around 10pm. If you arrive after
11pm be prepared to queue.

Old Compton Cafe
34 Old Compton Street Soho W1
Tel: 0171 439 3309
This is a very popular meeting place
for the clubbing fraternity. And here
in the heart of Soho meals are served
24 hours a day.

Calamity Jane's Restaurant
104 Heath Street Hampstead NW3
Telephone: 0171 435 2396
Open Mon-Thu and Sun until 2am;
Fri-Sat 3am
American- style hamburger joint,
loosely based on the folk legend.
The name derives from Calamity
Jane who used to drag-up in men's
clothing, shoot people, and go on wild
drinking binges. A favourite haunt for
North London insomniacs

Ranoush Juice Bar
43 Edgware Road W2
Tel: 0171 723 5929
Open daily 9am.-3am.
Far, far more than its name implies.
Fresh juices, of course. This Lebanese
establishment serves a wide selection
of Middle Eastern food .

Vingt Quatre
325 Fulham Road SW10.
Tel: 0171 376 7224
This 24 hour restaurant changed
hands some time ago but still attracts
the late night party revellers and
serious raconteurs. Despite the
radical change of image by the new
owners, it's still a great place for
eating breakfast three times a day,
although other dishes are on offer.

Yas
7 Hammersmith Road W14
Tel: 0171 603 9148
If you are on your way home from a
party, or a concert in Earls Court this
is not a bad place to make a pit stop.
This Arabian style bar/restaurant will
serve you alcohol until midnight, but
stays open for other munchies until
the crack-of-dawn.

Food Delivery
Room Service
The office is open daily until 1am,
Telephone: 0171 431 5555
Food delivered from 150 restaurants
from around the capital. Later
deliveries possible depending on
restaurant hours Mobile alcohol
license to deliver meals or wine and
beer. The cost is according to the
restaurant menu plus £4 delivery.
Internet order:www.room service. co.uk.

Gym
County Hall SE1
Tel: 0171 928 4900 (Members only)
The Club at County Hall
London's only all-night gym
-6,000sq ft fitness suite, 25-metre
pool, exercise studios, beauty spa, bar
and lounge.

Night Services

Flowers
Angela Saunders
London Hilton 22 Park Lane Wl
Tel: 0171 629 3355
Mon-Sat 9am-10pm
Perfect for that late-night kiss-and-make-up.

Darling Flowers
37 Theobalds Road WC1
Tel: 0171 404 8824/0181 697 7086
Orders taken 24 hours, late deliveries up to 11.30pm, but must be ordered before 6pm.

Interflora Flowerline
Tel:01529 304 545).
24-hour order line but deliveries only during office hours.

Gambling
If you fancy a flutter on the gaming tables you must join a casino well in advance. Most applications are processed, but it takes 48 hours (by law) for membership to be granted. If you're feeling lucky or time doesn't permit, you can always try and find an existing member to take you along as his/her guest- or if you are staying in a hotel, speak to your head porter.

Newspapers
If you want to find out what's happening in the world in advance, early editions of most newspapers can be purchased from around 9.30pm the night before. The best places are: The Trocadero, Piccadilly Circus, Marble Arch Station b2, 24 hour shops; all airports and main line train stations.

The streets in Queensway are finally empty.

Useful Information

For all your travel enquiries telephone the following numbers. If you have any difficulty contact the operator.

National operator	100
International:	155
Directory enquiries:	192
International enquiries	153

AIRPORTS

Gatwick:	01293 535353
Lost property:	01293 503162
Heathrow:	0181 759 4321
Lost property:	0181 745 7727
London City Airport:	0171 474 5555
Lost property:	0171 474 5555
Luton:	01582 405100
Lost property:	01582 405100
Stansted:	01279 680500
Lost property:	01279 502520

RAIL (24 HOUR SERVICES)

For all main line stations enquiries please telephone :   0345 484950

FOR LOST PROPERTY ENQUIRIES

Charing Cross:	0171 232 1070
Euston:	0171 922 6477
Kings Cross:	0171 922 9081
Liverpool Street:	0171 922 9158
Marylebone:	0990 165165
Paddington:	0171 313 1514
St Pancras:	0171 922 6478
Victoria:	0870 6030405
Waterloo:	0171 401 7861

London Regional Transport

24 hour daily service providing information on timetables, routes and all- night bus services   0171 222 1234

BREAKDOWN

AA:(Freephone)	0800 887766
National Breakdown:	01532 393434

Car Pounds and Declamping

Information: 0171 252 2222

A notice on the windowscreen informs you of the basic procedure.De clamping should take place between one and four hours from receiving payment but this is not guaranteed.The car can be re-clamped if it is not removed one hour after being de-clamped. Cars that are towed away are generally taken to the nearest car-pound. Telephone the above number to find out which pound.

LOST OR BROKEN CAR KEYS

Keys Galore 96 Gloucester Ave NW1 Tel: 0171 722 2731 Mobile number: 0836 798939 and ask for Matthew

24-Hour Petrol Stations

83 Park Lane W1	0171 499 6496
Texaco	
383 Edgware Rd W2	0171 723 9686
309 City Road EC1	0171 250 0052
Hampstead Rd NW1	0171 387 2326
161 Talgarth Rd W6	0181 741 5896

24-Hour Car Parks

Arlington Street W1	0171 499 3312
Young Street W8	0171 499 3265
Cadogan Place SW1	0171 235 5106

BLACK CABS

Computer Cab	0171 286 0286
Radio Taxi cabs	0171 272 0272
Dial-a-Cab	0171 253 5000
Lost property	0171 833 0996
Lady Cabs	0171 254 3501
COMPLAINTS	0171 230 1631

You will need to know the taxi drivers badge number

SELF DRIVE CAR HIRE

Avis	0181 848 8765
Budget	0171 935 3518
Europcar	0181 950 5050
Hertz	0990 996 699

LOST OR STOLEN CREDIT CARDS

Access	01702 354040
American Express	01273 696933
Barclaycard/	
Trustcard/ Visa	01604 230230
Diners Club	01252 513500
Freephone number	0800 460 800

EMERGENCY CASUALTIES:

Charing Cross Hospital
Fulham Palace Road W6
Tel: 0181 846 1234

Royal Free Hospital
Pond Street Hampstead NW3
Tel: 0171 794 0500

University College Hospital
Gower Street WC1
Tel: 0171 387 9300

St Mary's Hospital
Praed Street Paddington W2
Tel: 0171 725 6666

Moorfield Hospital
City Road EC1 (N.r Old Street Station)
Tel: 0171 253 3411
For emergency eye treatment.

CHEMISTS

Boots
114 Queensway W2
Tel: 0171 229 1183
Open daily until 10pm

Bliss
50-56 Willesden Lane NW6
Tel: 0171 624 8000 also at:
5-6 Marble Arch W1
Tel: 0171-723 6116
Open 365 days a year until midnight.

Zafash Pharmacy
233-235 Old Brompton Road SW5
Tel: 0171 373 2798. 24hours.

SOS DOCTORS
Tel: 0171-603 3332
24-hour visiting doctor. The costs are
£50 before midnight and £60 after.

24 HOUR AMBULANCE: MED CALL
Paramedical Service:
Tel: 0171 636 8282
Freephone: 0800 136 106

24-HOUR BUREAUX DE CHANGE
Chequepoint: 37 Coventry Street W1

POSTAL SERVICE
Late night Post office
24/28 William IV St Trafalgar Sq WC2
Tel: 0171 930 9580

Local and Late Night Radio Stations

Radio 1	**98.8fm**
Radio 2	88.91fm
Radio 3	**90.2-924fm**
Radio 4	92.4-94.6fm
Radio 5	**693-909am**
Classic FM	100-102fm
Capital Gold	**1548am**
Capital FM	95.8fm
Heart	**106.2fm**
Jazz FM	102.2fm
GLR	**94.9fm**
Kiss FM	100fm
LBC	**1152**
London News	97.3fm
Spectrum	**558am**
Virgin	105.8fm

Night Buses

N1 Archway - High Barnet

N2 Crystal Palace-
Trafalgar Sq North Finchley

N3 Victoria - Trafalgar Square
Beckenham -Chislehurst

N5 Trafalgar Sq Golders Green
- Edgware

N6 Aldwych - Trafalgar Square-
Kensal Rise

N8 Victoria -Trafalgar Sq - Bow

N9 Trafalgar Sq -Richmond -
Kingston

N11 Liverpool St. - Trafalgar Sq.
-Shepherd's Bush

N12 Shepherd's Bush -
Trafalgar Sq. - Dulwich

N84 Oxford Circus -Trafalgar Sq-
Nunhead

N13 Victoria -Trafalgar Sq. -
Potters Bar

N14. Trafalgar Sq. Kingston-
Chessington

N16 Victoria - Trafalgar Sq -
Kilburn - Edgware

N18 Trafalgar Sq Harrow Weald

N19 Clapham Junction -
Trafalgar Sq. - Finsbury Pk

N21 Trafalgar Sq - Cockfosters -
Potters Bar

N23 Liverpool St. - Trafalgar Sq.
Ealing Broadway

N26 Victoria-Hackney
Walthamstow

N29 Victoria-Wood Green-
Ponders End

N31 Camden Town-Kensington-
Camden Town.

N36 Trafalgar Sq -Lewisham -
Grove Park

N47 Victoria - Trafalgar Sq. -
Bromley - St Mary Cray

N51 Trafalgar Sq - Eltham -
Woolwich

N61 Trafalgar Sq -Eltham Sidcup

N52 Victoria -Trafalgar Sq
Willesden

N53 Victoria - Woolwich -Erith

N62 Victoria - Trafalgar Sq -
Eltham - Orpington

N72 Victoria - Trafalgar Sq -
Eltham - Welling

N68 Trafalgar Sq - Wimbledon -
Sutton

N70 Trafalgar Sq.- Surrey Quays
- Trafalgar Sq.

N71 Victoria -Trafalgar Sq. -
New Cross-Crystal Palace.

N72 See N62

N73 Victoria-Trafalgar Sq.-
Stoke Newington
Walthamstow

N76 Trafalgar Sq. -Leytonstone -
Hainault

N79 Oxford Circus -Trafalgar Sq
- Hither Green

N81 Trafalgar Sq- Bexleyheath -
Gillingham

N83 Victoria Station -Tottenham
- Wood Green

N84 See N12

N87 Trafalgar Sq. Streatham
or Hampton Court

N88 Trafalgar Sq - Sutton-
Croydon

N89 London Bridge Trafalgar Sq.
- Ruislip - Uxbridge

N90 Victoria - Trafalgar Sq
- Hammond Street

N91 Trafalgar Sq - Holloway -
Hornsey Rise

N 92 Victoria Station - Holloway
- North Finchley

N 93 Victoria - Trafalgar Sq -
Mount Pleasant -Hampstead

N 95 Victoria -Trafalgar Sq.-
East Ham - Dagenham

N 96 Trafalgar Sq.
Walthamstow - Debden

N 97 Trafalgar Sq-Hounslow -
Heathrow Airport or
Sunbury

N 98 Victoria - Trafalgar Sq.
Harold Hill

N 99 Trafalgar Sq.- Stanmore

N109 Aldwych - East Croydon -
New Addington

N134 Trafalgar Sq.- Muswell
Hill-
North Finchley

N139 Trafalgar Sq W. Hampstead

Index

Index

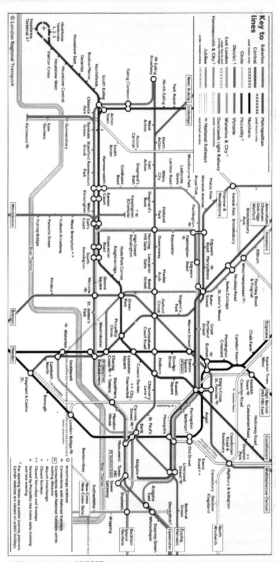